Military Response to UFO Activity

Cox

9310

Schiffer Books are available at special discounts for bulk purchases for sales promotions or premiums. Special editions, including personalized covers, corporate imprints, and excerpts can be created in large quantities for special needs. For more information contact the publisher:

Schiffer Publishing Ltd.
4880 Lower Valley Road
Atglen, PA 19310
Phone: (610) 593-1777; Fax: (610) 593-2002
E-mail: Info@schifferbooks.com

For the largest selection of fine reference books on this and related subjects, please visit our website at **www.schifferbooks.com**
We are always looking for people to write books on new and related subjects. If you have an idea for a book, please contact us at proposals@schifferbooks.com

This book may be purchased from the publisher. Include $5.00 for shipping. Please try your bookstore first. You may write for a free catalog.

In Europe, Schiffer books are distributed by
Bushwood Books
6 Marksbury Ave.
Kew Gardens
Surrey TW9 4JF England
Phone: 44 (0) 20 8392 8585; Fax: 44 (0) 20 8392 9876
E-mail: info@bushwoodbooks.co.uk
Website: www.bushwoodbooks.co.uk

Designed by Stephanie Daugherty
Type set in ITC American Typewriter/NewBskvll BT

ISBN: 978-0-7643-4062-8
Printed in the United States

Dedication

I dedicate this book to my family, who have always been there for me, and have never doubted my dreams, no matter how crazy they might seem. Also to anyone who finds themselves at a place in life where the question of *why* seems unanswerable, you are not alone.

For my parents, George B. and Helen A. Cox; they are the reason I am here. To James Bouck and Peter Robbins, for teaching me that great things are born from tiny sparks of inspiration and for giving me the inspiration to work on this exciting project.

Contents

Appendices

1

What Happens When Pilots in Military Jets Encounter a UFO?

Air Force pilots on almost every continent find they are coming face to face with something utterly impossible, *but* yet it is very real. If military pilots fire on an object, they do it in an act of self-defense. Some countries are starting to admit there's a problem in our skies – France for instance, who through the COMETA Report, has publicly admitted UFOs' existence and the dangers in our skies and to our national security.

There seems to be an agreement at the highest levels of the military around the world that UFOs or UAPs (Unidentified Aerial Phenomenon) are not aggressive; even when provoked, they do not retaliate for the most part.

Have military pilots ever fired upon a UFO? Surprisingly the answer is *yes*. In 1976, an Iranian Air Force Major was ordered to man his F4 II Phantom jet and intercept a UAP over Tehran; every time he went to fire a sidewinder missile the equipment malfunctioned.

In 1980, a lieutenant in the Peruvian Air Force[1] (Spanish: Fuerza Aérea del Perú, abbreviated FAP is the branch of the Peruvian Armed Forces) was tasked with defending the nation and its interests through the use of air power, was asked to intercept an aerial Spy device. The UAP was a balloon-looking object; the pilot fired a barrage of machine gun bullets at the object with no effect. The pilot then tried to lock on the UAP with missiles, three times. Each time, at the last second, the object shot straight up in the air. Soldiers and staff at the LaJoya Military Base (approximately 1,800) witnessed the event.

Are UFOs a national security threat? According to the United States Air Force, the answer is *no*, but why do they threaten some witnesses about going public with what they have seen? Still, are they a risk of national security? That's a real question that remains a secret within the military. Take the United States Air Force for example. There are claims that there are no such things as UFOs. Let's look at the Official Website for the United States Air Force.

Unidentified Flying Objects and Air Force Project Blue Book²

Date Posted 10/17/2005

From 1947 to 1969, the United States Air Force investigated Unidentified Flying Objects under Project Blue Book. The project, headquartered at Wright-Patterson Air Force Base, Ohio, was terminated December 17, 1969. Of a total of 12,618 sightings reported to Project Blue Book, 701 remained "unidentified."

The decision to discontinue UFO investigations was based on an evaluation of a report prepared by the University of Colorado entitled, "Scientific Study of Unidentified Flying Objects," a review of the University of Colorado's report by the National Academy of Sciences, previous UFO studies, and Air Force experience investigating UFO reports during 1940 to 1969.

As a result of these investigations, studies and experience gained from investigating UFO reports since 1948, the conclusions of Project Blue Book were:

No UFO reported, investigated and evaluated by the Air Force was ever an indication of threat to our national security.

There was no evidence submitted to or discovered by the Air Force that sightings categorized as "unidentified" represented technological developments or principles beyond the range of modern scientific knowledge; and there was no evidence indicating that sightings categorized as "unidentified" were extraterrestrial vehicles.

With the termination of Project Blue Book, the Air Force regulation establishing and controlling the program for investigating and analyzing UFOs was rescinded. Documentation regarding the former Blue Book investigation was permanently transferred to the Modern Military Branch, National Archives and Records Service, and is available for public review and analysis.

Since the termination of Project Blue Book, nothing has occurred that would support a resumption of UFO investigations by the Air Force. Given the current environment of steadily decreasing defense budgets, it is unlikely the Air Force would become involved in such a costly project in the foreseeable future.

There are a number of universities and professional scientific organizations that have considered UFO phenomena during periodic meetings and seminars. A list of private organizations interested in aerial phenomena may be found in Encyclopedia of Associations, published by Gale Research.[3] Interest in and timely review of UFO reports by private groups ensures that sound evidence is not overlooked by the scientific community. Persons wishing to report UFO sightings should be advised to contact local law enforcement agencies.

UFOs having vast superior technology with unknown agendas is a frightening prospect, even if the pilot feels the need to fire upon an object out of self-defense; such actions could have devastating consequences.

A group of former Air Force officers gathered to go public with an assertion they have kept mostly under wraps for decades: that UFOs visited the bases they were stationed at and caused nuclear weapons systems to temporarily malfunction. The group, convened by UFO researcher Robert Hastings, came to the National Press Club in Washington to discuss their individual experiences and to urge a government that tried to ignore and silence them when they came forward years ago to finally come clean.

Hastings said he believes that visitors from outer space are fixating on nuclear weapons because they want to send a message:

Disarm Before the World Destroys Itself

Robert Salas, a former missile launch officer at Malmstrom Air Force Base[4], said that ten nuclear missiles were suddenly and inexplicably disabled in March 1967 at the Montana installation after members of his flight security team saw a "large glowing, pulsating red oval-shaped object" about thirty to forty feet in diameter hovering over the front gate. When he reported the incident to his superiors the next day, he was told to keep quiet.

"What you read today is evidence of a true real phenomenon. It sounds fantastic, and it is fantastic," said Salas, after he and his fellow officers from other bases in the Western US shared similar accounts. The government, Salas said, is...

...deliberately withholding the facts, continuously since 1969 and, by doing so, do not allow the people of this country to engage in the decision regarding events that are clearly a national security issue for concern for all of us. We're simply asking for the truth.

As mentioned, from 1947 to 1969, the Air Force investigated unidentified flying objects under what was called Project Blue Book. Of a total of 12,618 sightings under the program, 701 remained "unidentified." The military discontinued the program after consulting with scientists and concluding that none of the objects posed a threat to national security or could be identified as "extraterrestrial."

When asked to comment on the new assertions, an Air Force spokeswoman cited a 2005 fact sheet that said:

Since the termination of Project Blue Book, nothing has occurred that would support a resumption of UFO investigations.

Hastings said he has heard of a UFO incident occurring at Malmstrom as recently as 2007. The declassified documents Hastings presented at the news conference include decades-old government memos detailing reports of sightings of objects in the skies above Alabama, Montana, New Mexico, and North Dakota.

"The American people have a right to know the facts," Hastings told reporters. "This is a national security issue but it is (also) a need-to-know issue, a right-to-know issue. Citizens in every country on Earth should be let in on this secret."

Hastings said he has talked to 120 former or retired US military personnel about the presence of UFOs at nuclear weapons sites across the United States and around the globe as early as 1945, when the world entered the nuclear age with the bombings of Hiroshima and Nagasaki. For some of the officers who came forward, going public wasn't easy.

Bruce Fenstermacher, a missile combat crew commander at F.E. Warren Air Force Base in Cheyenne, Wyoming, was "laughed at" by superiors when he reported a UFO sighting at a launch site that one of his sergeants had passed on to him, he said. He decided to keep his head low after that.

"I was very careful about who I told what," he said. "I was concerned. I don't want to be considered a kook. But I think it's more important to come out and tell our story."

2

Engagement Over Peru

Date: April 11, 1980

Time: 0715

Location: Fuerza Aerea Peruana, La Joya, Peru

GPS: 16 Deg 47 Min 30.23 Sec South   71Deg 53Min 11.20 Sec West

Elevation: 3894 Feet

Witnesses: Approximately 1600 - 1800

Main Witness: Lt. Oscar Santa María Huertas, Pilot, P.A.F.

Details of UFO / UAP Event:[5, 6] On the morning of 11 April 1980, personnel from the Air Force of Peru (Fuerza Aerea Peruana (FAP) base in La Joya, Peru, 621.3 miles south of the Peruvian capital, detected a strange object flying in the vicinity. Described as a blued dome, looking like a light bulb split in half, with a wide metal base that made everything shine. When he approached and saw it completely, he realized that it lacked nozzles, wings, windows, antennas...had nothing at all. It was a very smooth surface above and below."

As a member of the military, what were you and the base commander thinking?

Assuming that the intruder was a spy aircraft, the base commander ordered an immediate scramble of a Sukhoi SU-22 fighter-bomber with orders to destroy the target, originally supposed to be a sort of Aerial Spy Device located 3 miles away. The time was 7:15 a.m. and base personnel – a complement of some 1800 men were in formation, witnessing this event.

Note: 3 miles away would be the city of La Joya, Peru from the air strip.

You, being a member of the Air Force, what were your intentions?

Oscar Santa María Huertas, a lieutenant in the FAP, piloted the aircraft that raced down the runway on an intercept-and-destroy mission. When the object was within his sights, suspended and motionless some 1800 feet AGL [above ground level], Lt. Santa María pulled the trigger, firing a hail of bullets from his aircraft's 30mm guns. Sixty-four rounds out of a total of 160 were fired at the UFO. The rounds appeared to pierce the object without exploding or causing any harm. The object then flew itself skyward at a tremendous speed, chased by the SU-22.

What happened next?

The UFO then gained speed. Lt. Santa María ignited the afterburners, propelling the Sukhoi to Mach 1.2, breaking the sound barrier.

Was the object picked up on radar?

Up to that moment, the object had not been detected by radar. For this reason, the pilot, Lt. Santa Maria, did not consider the plane's missiles. He only sought to get close enough to the object to fire again, having over 100 rounds left.

What happened when you got close to the UFO for the second time?

When the SU-22 was in range of the UFO, I tried on three different occasions to lock on to the target with my missiles; all three times the object made a sudden stop, violating the laws of inertia (see Appendix A "Newton's Law of Motion"). The fighter-bomber flew past it, with both vehicles at an altitude of 36,000 feet, the object pulled away quickly, and gaining altitude at the same time. Later, it stopped abruptly, and he had to maneuver to avoid colliding with it.

Did you ever feel like you were in danger chasing the object?

It was then that he (Lt. Santa María) and his aircraft went from being hunters to prey. He was being pursued by the Unidentified Flying Object at 62,000 feet, nearly 3000 feet beyond the aircraft manufacturer's specifications. Furthermore, his fuel supply was running low.

Faced with this situation, Oscar Santa María decided to abandon his mission and withdraw, even as the UFO continued to ascend, losing itself in space. He was 52 miles away from his base, and 22 minutes had elapsed since his first contact with the UFO. After landing, the UFO reappeared, remaining visible to the air base for nearly two hours.

Can you describe the object that you were chasing?

The object (that Lt. Santa María attacked) was described as an object with a blued dome, looking like a light bulb split in half, with a wide metal base that made everything shine. When I approached and saw it completely, I realized that it lacked nozzles, wings, windows, antenna...nothing at all. It was a very smooth surface above and below."

The Aircraft Lt. Santa Maria Used: The Sukhoi SU-22.

The SU-22 was designed as a high speed, medium range, low level ground attack rescue aircraft. Its origin can be traced back to the basic SU-7 aircraft of the 1950s; the design was continuously developed, emerging as the variable geometry (Swing-wing 30:63) SU-17 / 22, the most modern and powerful Warsaw Pact fighter bomber. The NATO code name for the type was "Fitter."

Origin: Russia

Type: single-seat ground-attack fighter

Max Speed: 1,198 kt/1,380 mph Mach 2.09 at altitude above 40,000 feet

Max Range: 675 km / 419 miles

Dimensions: span 13.80 m / 45 feet, 3 inches. Weapons: AAMs, ASMs, guided bombs, bombs, cluster bombs, dispenser weapons, napalm tanks, large-caliber rockets, rocket-launcher pods. Cannon pods, drop tanks and ECM pods, carried on nine external hard points

Length: 18.75 m / 61 ft 6.2 in height 5.00 m / 16 ft 5 in.[6]

Weight: empty 95,00kg / 20,944 lb max. Take-off 19,500 kg / 42,990 lb

Power plant: one 11,250 kg (24,802 lb.) afterburning thrust Lyul'ka AL-21F-3 turbojet

Armament: two 30-mm NR-30 with 80 rounds per gun; provision for 4,250 kg (9,370 Ib) of disposable stores, including tactical nuclear

A Sukhoi SU-22 fighter-bomber.

At the time, the La Joya Air Base was considered one of the most strategic and secret in Peru due to its proximity to the Chilean border, a country against which a war was nearly unleashed years earlier. The base had underground facilities in the desert pampas, where valuable combat aircraft were concealed.

Here is a memo received by the Department of Defense, Joint Chief of Staff:

```
PARANET CLASSIFICATION NUMBER: P 1005-1 PE
DEPARTMENT OF DEFENSE
JOINT CHIEFS OF STAFF
MESSAGE CENTER


VZCZCMLT565        7YUW
MULT               18134
ACTION
  DIA[?]
DISTR
    IADB(01)  J5(02) J3:NMCC NIDS SECDEF(07) SECDEF:
USDP(15)
    ATSD:AE(01) ASD:PA&E(01) ::DIA(20) NMIC
-   CMC CC WASHINGTON DC
-   CSAF WASHINGTON DC
-   CNO WASHINGTON DC

-   CSA WASHINGTON DC
-   CIA WASHINGTON DC
-   SFCSTATE WASHINGTON DC
-   NSA WASH DC
    FILF
(047)
TRANSIT/1542115/1542207/000:52TOR1542204
DE RUESLMA #4888 1542115
ZNY CCCCC
R 0220527 JUN 80
FM USDAO LIMA PERU
TO RUEKJCS/DIA WASHDC
INFO RULPALJ/USCINCSO QUARRY HT8 PN
RULPAFA/USDAFSO HOWARD AFB PN
BT
SUBJ: IR 6 876 0146 80 (U)
```

THIS IS AN INFO REPORT, NOT FINALLY EVAL INTEL

1. (U) CTRY: PERU (PE)
2. TITLE (U) UFO SIGHTED IN PERU (U)
3. (U) DATE OF INFO: 800510
4. (U) ORIG: USDAO AIR LIMA PERU
5. (U) REQ REFS: Z-D13-PE030
6. (U) SOURCE: 6 876 0138. OFFICER IN THE PERUVAIAN AIR FORCE WHO OBSERVED THE EVENT AND IS IN A POSITION TO BE PARTY TO CONVERSATION CONCERNING THE EVENT. SOURCE HAS REPORTED RELIABILITY IN THE PAST.
7. SUMMARY: SOURCE REPORTED THAT A UFO WAS SPOTTED ON TWO DIFFERENT OCCASIONS NEAR PERUVIAN AIR FORCE (FAP) BASE IN SOUTHERN PERU. THE FAP TRIED TO INTERCEPT AND DESTROY THE UFO, BUT WITHOUT SUCCESS.

PAGE 1   001001111
PAGE 2

8A. DETAILS: SOURCE TOLD RO ABOUT THE SPOTTING OF AN UNIDENTIFIED FLYING OBJECT IN THE VICINITY OF MARIANO MALGAR AIR BASE, LA JOYA, PERU (168058, 0715306W). SOURCE STATED THAT THE VEHICLE WAS SPOTTED ON TWO DIFFERENT OCCASIONS. THE FIRST WAS DURING THE MORNING HOURS OF 9 MAY 80, AND THE SECOND DURING THE EARLY EVENING HOURS OF 10 MAY 80.

SOURCE STATED THAT ON 9 MAY, WHILE A GROUP OF FAP OFFICERS WERE IN FORMATION AT MARIANO MALGAR. THEY SPOTTED A UFO THAT WAS ROUND IN SHAPE, HOVERING NEAR THE AIRFIELD. THE AIR COMMANDER SCRAMBLED AN SU-22 AIRCRAFT TO MAKE AN INTERCEPT. THE PILOT, ACCORDING TO A THIRD PARTY, INTERCEPTED THE VEHICLE AND FIRED UPON IT AT VERY CLOSE RANGE WITHOUT CAUSING ANY APPARENT DAMAGE. THE PILOT TRIED TO MAKE A SECOND PASS ON THE VEHICLE, BUT THE UFO OUT-RAN THE SU-22.
THE SECOND SIGHTING WAS DURING HOURS OF DARKNESS. THE VEHICLE WAS LIGHTED. AGAIN AN SU-22 WAS SCRAMBLED, BUT THE VEHICLE OUT-RAN THE AIRCRAFT.

8B. DIRG CMTS: RO HAS HEARD DISCUSSION ABOUT THE SIGHTING FROM OTHER SOURCES. APPARENTLY SOME

VEHICLE WAS SPOTTED, BUT ITS ORIGIN REMAINS UNKNOWN.

9. (U) PROJ NO: N/A
10. (U) COLL MGMT CODES: AB
11. (U) SPEC INST: NONE. DIRC: NO.
12. (U) PREP BY: NORMAN H. RUNGE, COL. AIRA
13. (U) APP BY: VAUGHN E. WILSON, CAPT. DATT, ALUSNA
14. (U) REQ EVAL: NO REL TO: NONE
15. (U) ENCL: N/A
16. (U) DIST BY ORIG: N/A
BT
#4888
ANNOTES
JAL 117

PAGE 2
000101111
NNNN
0222087
[END REPORT]

See Appendix A Department of Defense memos regarding this incident.

3

Engagement Over Tehran[8,9]

Date: September 19, 1976

Time: 0030

Location: 40 nautical miles (74 km) north of Tehran

GPS: 35 Deg 41 Min 43.48 Sec North   51Deg 25 Min 26.38 Sec East

Elevation: 3857 Feet

Witnesses: Captain Mohammad Reza Azizkhani

Main Witness: Major Parviz Jafari

Details of UFO / UAP Event: 19 September 1976, the Imperial Iranian Air Force command post at Tehran received four reports by telephone, from civilians in the Shemiran city district, of unusual activity in the night sky. These calls came in quick succession.

I have heard a lot about the dogfight over Tehran, so I started investigating this sighting as I would with any other report (minus contact information). I started searching the Internet and reading books; one of the best books I have read on the subject is by Leslie Kean, *UFO's General, Pilots and Government Officials Go On Record*.[7] I started jotting down notes and the next thing I knew I had six pages of tidbits regarding the dogfight over Tehran. I have noticed a lot of facts that didn't coincide with the majority of the information. Leslie Kean had a great opportunity; she interviewed the pilot in November 2007. The pilot was Major Parviz Jafari, now a retired General with the Iranian Air Force.

Why was there a UFO the size of a jetliner hovering north of Tehran during the early morning hours of September 19, 1976?

Questions we should be asking ourselves:

- Is this a technological device?

- Is it from a higher intelligence Being?

- What was their reason for being there?

- What was the purpose?

- Where did this technology come from?

- Do they come in peace?

The Iranian military seemed baffled by what happened that night. They sent two of the finest attack jets in the world at the time, only to come back to Shahrokhi AFB, empty handed, frightened, and confused as to what the object could be. The report of the strange encounter was taken by an American colonel, and was circulated amongst the highest levels of the US government, including the National Security Agency (NSA). There are several aspects to this case that make it particularly outstanding:

- Unconventional movement of the object

- Unconventional lights associated with the object

- High amount of witnesses, including extremely credible military sources

- Radar returns from the air and ground

- Possible electromagnetic pulse (EMP) weaponry used by the object on the F4

- Smaller object(s) that seemingly detach from the primary object which also have unconventional movement and lighting

Note: What is EMP weaponry? An electromagnetic pulse is a burst of electromagnetic radiation. The abrupt pulse of electromagnetic radiation usually results from certain types of high energy explosions, especially a nuclear explosion, or from a suddenly fluctuating magnetic field. The resulting rapidly changing electric fields and magnetic fields may couple with electrical/electronic systems to produce damaging current and voltage surges.

What were the first events surrounding this UFO?

At approximately 0030 hours local time (2100Z), 19 September 1976, the Imperial Iranian Air Force command post at Tehran received four reports by telephone, from civilians in the Shemiran city district, of unusual activity in the night sky. Some callers reported seeing a bird-like object; others reported a helicopter with a bright light.

When the command post found no helicopters airborne to account for the reports, they called General Yousefi, assistant deputy commander of operations. General Yousefi at first said the object was only a star, but after conferring with the control tower at Mehrabad International Airport and then looking for himself to see a very bright object larger than a star, he decided to scramble one F-4 Phantom II jet fighter from Shahrokhi Air Force Base in Hamadan, approximately 175 miles west of Tehran.

What happened next?

At 0130 hours the F-4, piloted by Captain Mohammad Reza Azizkhani was launched and proceeded to a point 40 nautical miles (74 km) north of Tehran 36Deg 16 Min 19.20 Sec North, 51 Deg 25 Min 13.54 Sec East. Above the Golestanak Mountains. It was noted that the object was of such brilliance that it could be seen from 70 miles (110 km) away. When the aircraft approached to approximately 25 nautical miles (46 km) from the object, the jet suddenly lost all instrumentation and communication capabilities, prompting Azizkhani to break off the pursuit and turn back to Shahrohki Air Force Base; both systems resumed functioning when the pilot broke off the engagement.

Was another aircraft deployed to assist in bringing down the object?

A second F-4 was sent at 0140 hours and the Major Parviz Jafari acquired a radar lock 27 miles at a 12 o'clock position, at a speed of 150 knots. When he got within 25 miles, the UFO reacted and was able to jump 25 miles away from the approaching aircraft; this was evident on radar as well.

Did you ever feel threatened while you were chasing the object?

A second but smaller object detached itself from the first object, and advanced towards Jafari's F-4 at high speed. Jafari thought this object was trying to attack him, so he tried to launch a sidewinder missile. However, he couldn't do so because the plane's instruments suddenly didn't work, including the instruments needed to fire the missile and all communication. Jafari tried to eject himself from the plane but the ejector equipment didn't work either.

Jafari then tried to escape the object by turning his plane sharply. The object followed behind the plane for a short time, about 7 kilometers back, then turned and rejoined the bigger object. As was the case with the first F-4 that had been sent up, the instruments in the second F-4 that hadn't been working, began again working after the second object flew away.

Since the object remained one step ahead of you what happened next?

Suddenly, according to the supervisor, the object seemed to disappear, and then suddenly to re-appear a mile further, just seconds later. It appeared this time as bright as the sun. It was all yellow, like a star, but much bigger. Then it appeared to change shape, and the colors of the lights appeared to be blue, orange, red, and yellow. Jafari couldn't make out its size or structure because of its intense brilliance. He described its lights as like flashing strobe lights, which formed a diamond shape.

Did the object do anything else that seemed strange?

Jafari then saw another brightly lit object detach itself from the other side of the original (the first). It dropped straight down at high speed, then came to rest on the ground below. Jafari said it was so bright that it lit up the ground and the rocks around it. The F-4, at a lower altitude, flew over where the object had landed. Jafari's navigator marked the position where it had touched down.

What seemed to be the problem?

A problem for Jafari was that the object kept changing position with such suddenness that he couldn't track it. Jafari estimated that each jump in the object's position was 10 degrees, representing about 12 kilometers.

So you broke off the attack; what happened next?

The F-4 headed for Mehrabad Airport where it would land. However, on final approach, Jafari saw yet another bright cylinder-shaped object, which had bright steady lights on each end, and a flashing light in the middle. This object flew over the F-4. The control tower at Mehrabad reported no other aircraft in the area, but tower personnel were able to see the object when given directions by Jafari. Shortly afterwards, the object also flew over the control tower; at that moment, all the electronic instrumentation in the tower ceased to work until after the object had passed.

Jafari landed his plane at Mehrabad. He and his navigator said that each time they had passed through a magnetic bearing of 150 degrees from Mehrabad, the plane experienced interference and communications failure, of the sort which a civilian airliner also experienced when it passed through this same magnetic bearing.

What happened when you landed?

The next day, Jafari and his F-4 navigator flew by helicopter to the site where they had seen the smaller object land. In the daylight they saw that it was a dry lake bed, but they saw no traces of the object. The helicopter circled the area to the west, where its radio picked up a noticeable beeper signal, which was loudest near some small houses. The helicopter landed, and Jafari asked the residents if they had seen anything strange the previous night. They said they had heard a sound after midnight. That was all.

Note: **The Tehran UFO incident has features common to many UFO cases:**

- **The malfunctioning electrical systems of the two F-4 interceptors.** Over past years, there have been nearly 200 reports by pilots who said their planes experienced electromagnetic disturbances when strange objects flew near, but that everything in the plane returned to normal when the strange objects flew off.

- **The involvement of American military personnel, and the reaction of the US government.** Major Jafari said that those who were at the meeting, in which he briefed his superiors about his experience, included an American colonel with the US Military Advisory and Assistance Group in Tehran, who was taking notes.

- **The reaction of UFO debunkers.** One of the best known debunkers, Philip J. Klass, said that what was seen was probably Jupiter, and that pilot incompetence accounted for the equipment malfunction. However, Jupiter's position in the sky on that night was far away from the position in the sky where the UFO was seen. Also, the UFO performed maneuvers in the sky which Jupiter just could not.

The American Defense Intelligence Agency (DIA) was most impressed by this UFO incident. The DIA drew up a report which it distributed to the White House, the Secretary of State, the Joint Chiefs of Staff, the NSA and the Central Intelligence Agency (CIA).

The report said that this incident was a classic which met all the criteria needed for a valid study of the UFO phenomenon. What makes it a classic for the criteria?

1. The objects had been seen by many witnesses in different locations, both from the air and from the ground;

2. The credibility of many of the witnesses was high, since they included an Air Force general, qualified aircrews, and experienced tower operators; visual sightings were confirmed by radar; similar electromagnetic effects (EME) were reported by three separate aircraft; some crew members suffered physiological effects, like loss of night vision due to the brightness of the object; and,

3. The objects showed an inordinate maneuverability.

Another report surfaced, this time from the American embassy in Rabat, Morocco, to the US State Department. It said:

...that many people from many locations in Morocco had seen a similar object three or four hours after the incident over Tehran. It flew quite low along the Atlantic coast. It appeared disc-shaped, but looked more tube-like from closer up.

However, the response of the State Department was that all UFOs could be attributed to natural causes and that no further study was warranted. This would be expected, this having been the official US position on UFOs since 1969. No matter how compelling the evidence that objects like the one over Tehran are intelligently controlled, and that the controllers are not of Earth, governments in the world over – and particularly the US government as the world's self-appointed policeman – have no choice but to go into denial, for fear that their authority would dissipate.

Despite the US government's official attitude, the Shah of Iran (this was before the Iranian Revolution) took an interest in this UFO incident. He visited Sharokhi air base and called a meeting attended by generals and by the pilots who had been involved. The Shah asked Jafari what he thought about what he'd encountered. Jafari replied that the objects could not have been from our planet, so amazing were the things they were able to do. The Shah simply said "yes", and told Jafari that this wasn't the first time he had received such reports.

Just as the official position of the US government on all UFOs is to be expected, so the position of reflexive UFO debunkers on all UFOs is equally to be expected. If UFO debunkers didn't debunk all UFOs, including the one over Tehran, then they wouldn't be UFO debunkers. It's just what they do.

4

Malmstrom
Air Force Base, Montana

(3-16-1967)

This is the story of events that happened in 1967 to Strategic Air Command (SAC) Missile Combat Officers – missile technicians assigned to operate the Minuteman Intercontinental Ballistic Missile, an essential part of America's Cold War strategic nuclear deterrent.[12, 13, 14]

In the middle of Montana on March 16, 1967, it was a beautiful Thursday morning; temperatures ranged from 1 degree to 10 degrees, with 84 percent humidity; winds were from the NNW at 6 mph with gusts of 10 mph, with visibility at 7 miles, with fog and light snow.

A 24' wide by 8' tall video wall with 9,562 by 3,072 resolution. *Photo courtesy of ©2010 CineMassive™.*

The E-Flight Missile Combat Crew was below ground in the Echo-Flight Launch Control Center (LCC) or capsule. During the early morning hours, several reports came in from security patrols and maintenance crews that they had seen UFOs. The UFO that was reported was directly above one of the E-Flight Launch Facilities (LF) or silos. It turned out that at least one security policeman was so frightened by this encounter that he never again returned to security duty.

A short time later, Robert Salas, Deputy Crew Commander (DMCCC) and a 1ˢt Lieutenant, was briefing the Crew Commander (MCCC), a Captain, on the flight status when the alarm horn sounded. Over the next half-minute, all ten of their missiles reported a "No-Go" condition. One by one across the board, each missile had became inoperable.

From there on, as an ex-Missile Technician describes it: "All Hell broke loose!" Among the many calls to and from the E-Flight LCC, one was to the MCCC of November-Flight which links to the equally dramatic story of what happened in another LCC that same morning.

In this case we have a shutdown of strategic nuclear missiles coincident with UFO sighting over a missile silo! These were missiles lost to America's nuclear deterrent forces.

The following section is as told by Robert Salas who was the DMCCC in N-Flight that morning. He says:

> My recollection is that, while on duty as a Deputy Missile Combat Crew Commander below ground in the LCC, during the morning hours of 16 March 1967, I received a call from the Non-Commissioned Officer (NCO) in charge of Launch Control Center site security.
>
> He said that he and other guards had observed unidentified flying objects in the vicinity which had flown over the LCC a few times. He could only distinguish them as "lights" at that time. I did not take this report seriously and directed him to keep observing and report back if anything more significant happened. I believed this first call to be a joke.
>
> A few minutes later, the security NCO called again. This time he was clearly frightened and was shouting his words:
>
> "Sir, there's one hovering outside the front gate!"
>
> "One what?"
>
> "A UFO! It's just sitting there. We're all just looking at it. What do you want us to do?"
>
> "What? What does it look like?"
>
> "I can't really describe it. It's glowing red. What are we supposed to do?"

"Make sure the site is secure and I'll phone the Command Post."

"Sir, I have to go now; one of the guys just got injured."

Before I could ask about the injury, he was off the line. I immediately went over to my commander, Lt. Fred Meiwald, who was on a scheduled sleep period. I woke him and began to brief him about the phone calls and what was going on topside. In the middle of this conversation, we both heard the first alarm klaxon resound through the confined space of the capsule, and both immediately looked over at the panel of annunciated lights at the Commander's station. A "No-Go" light and two red security lights were lit indicating problems at one of our missile sites. Fred jumped up to query the system to determine the cause of the problem. Before he could do so, another alarm went off at another site, then another and another simultaneously. Within the next few seconds, we had lost six to eight missiles to a "No-Go" (inoperable) condition.

None of the four or five missiles which faulted came back on line. Some signal had been sent to the missiles which caused them to go off alert status. After reporting this incident to the Command Post, I phoned the Security Station. He said that the man who had approached the UFO had not been injured seriously but was being evacuated by helicopter to the base. Once topside, I spoke directly with the security guard about the UFOs. He added that the UFO had a red glow and appeared to be saucer shaped. He repeated that it had been immediately outside the front gate, hovering silently.

We sent a security patrol to check our LFs after the shutdown, and they reported sighting another UFO during that patrol. They also lost radio contact with our site immediately after reporting the UFO. We were relieved by our scheduled replacement crew later that morning. The missiles had still not been brought on line by on-site maintenance teams. Again, UFOs were sighted by security personnel at or about the time Minuteman Strategic missiles shutdown.

Investigation Process of the E-Flight and Strategic Missile Laboratory

An in-depth investigation of the E-Flight incident was undertaken. Full scale on-site and laboratory tests at Boeing's Seattle plant were conducted. Both declassified Strategic Missile Wing documents and interviews with Boeing engineers who conducted tests following the E-Flight Incident investigation confirm that no cause for the missile shutdowns was ever found.

The most that could be done was to reproduce the effects by directly introducing a 10-volt pulse onto a data line. One conclusion was that the only way this could be done from outside the shielded system was through an electromagnetic pulse from an unknown source.

Is our National Security at risk?

During the events of that morning in 1967, UFOs were sighted by security personnel at the November Flight LCC, at one N-Flight LF, and by other security personnel at Echo-Flight LFs. These sightings were reported separately to the capsule crews at both LCCs at or about the same time Minuteman Strategic missiles shut down at both sites.

US Air Force has confirmed that Echo flights' entire missiles shutdown within ten seconds of each other and that no cause for this could be found. For many years, the Air Force has maintained that no reported UFO incident has ever affected national security. It is established fact that a large number of Air Force personnel reported sighting UFOs at the time many of our strategic missiles became unable to launch.

Do you think the incidents described above had national security implications? In one previously classified message, SAC Headquarters described the E-Flight incident as: loss of strategic alert of all ten missiles within ten seconds of each other for no apparent reason and a "...cause for grave concern... (To SAC headquarters)." (Emphasis ours.) There is a great discrepancy between the United States Air Force's public position relative to UFOs and national security, and the established facts of this case.

Were there other sightings around the same time?

According to articles from the *Great Falls Tribune* newspaper, on February 8, 1967, Louis DeLeon saw two strange objects in the sky which did not look like airplanes and they glowed an orange and red color while driving east of Chester, Montana. Later, ten miles east of Chester, Jake Walkman was awakened by a bright light at his home. From his back yard, he sighted a "flying saucer"-shaped object. The next evening, George Kawanishi, a foreman for the Great Northern Railroad, saw a bright ball of light in the sky directly above the Chester train depot. These are but a few of the sightings which preceded the missile shutdown incidents later in March. It was during this same period, according to Col. Don Crawford (USAF retired), that a two-person SAT, assigned to Echo Flight, was performing a routine check of the missile launch facilities a few miles north of Lewistown, Montana. As they approached one of the launch facilities, an astonishing sight caused the driver to slam on his brakes. Stunned in amazement, they watched as, about 300 feet ahead, a very large glowing object hovered silently directly over the launch facility. One of them picked up Command Post to report it. The officer on duty at the Command Post refused to accept the report and simply stated, "We no longer record those kinds of reports," indicating he didn't want to hear about the UFO. Crawford, unsure of what to tell his shaken security guard, decided to give the guard his permission to fire his weapon at the object if it seemed hostile.

"Thanks, sir, but I really don't think it would do any good."
A few seconds later, the object silently flew away.

There were sightings in the area before and after the missile shutdown incidents by military personnel and civilians.

Via his VHF hand microphone, the security guard called then Captain Don Crawford, who was the DMCCC on duty that evening.

"Sir, you wouldn't believe what I'm looking at," said the security guard.

He described what they were seeing. Crawford didn't believe him at first but the young airman insisted he was telling the truth, his voice revealing his emotional state.

Eventually, Crawford took him seriously enough to call the base commander regarding the sighting, explaining the command post would not take the report from the two witnesses who worked base security.

5

What Do Military Officials Around the World Say About UFOs?

(Including Our Own Air Force Who Stated Publicly
That "UFOs Do Not Exist?"[15, 16])

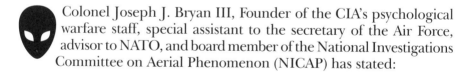 Colonel Joseph J. Bryan III, Founder of the CIA's psychological warfare staff, special assistant to the secretary of the Air Force, advisor to NATO, and board member of the National Investigations Committee on Aerial Phenomenon (NICAP) has stated:

> These UFOs are interplanetary devices systematically observing the earth, either manned or under remote control, or both.

And:

> Information on UFOs, including sighting reports, has been and is still being officially withheld.

Sergeant-Major Robert O. Dean, former NATO intelligence analyst for SHAPE (Supreme Headquarters Allied Powers Europe) made...a recommendation to General Limnitzer, the American four-star general that he worked for. And they suggested this is so sensitive...

The conclusions that we have reached, we believe could be... substantially earthshaking to the people unless they're prepared for it. We believe at this point that this should be given the highest classification NATO has [which] at that time was and still is Cosmic Top Secret.

From a videotaped interview in which Dean discussed SHAPE's alleged report entitled "An Assessment" based on a three-year investigation of UFOs being tracked on radar over central Europe:

Wright Patterson Air Force Base...was the headquarters for the foreign technology division of the US Air Force. It later became the headquarters for the alien technology division of the US Air Force. Wright Patterson, for many, many years was the central repository of not only the hardware, but some of the little bodies and even some of the living crew members who had been retrieved. But it became very clear after a time that there wasn't enough room at Wright Patterson Air Force Base. We literally filled up hangar after hangar with hardware. We're storing it now in at least three different Air Force bases and much of it is being kept underground at a place not too far from Las Vegas just beyond Nellis Air Force Base which is repeatedly referred to as Dreamland, Groom Lake, or Site 51. That, today is one of the biggest repositories of hardware.

From a live national broadcast on CBS in 1958, Major Donald E. Keyhoe, USMC stated:

The Air Force had put out a secret order for its pilots to capture UFOs.... For the last six months we have been working with a congressional committee investigating official secrecy concerning proof that UFOs are real machines under intelligent control.

Keyhoe had an approved script to follow, but when he deviated unexpectedly from it with this astonishing statement, the audio was cut-off in the middle of his sentence, "for reasons of national security."

Steve Lewis, former Air Force intelligence officer who spent many years investigating the UFO phenomenon for the US military made a statement after his retirement when he announced that he was convinced UFOs were intelligently controlled, extraterrestrial vehicles. He would give no further details of his work, but said "that very little of the information in possession of the military had been released." Further, "That the movie *Close Encounters of the Third Kind* is more realistic than you can believe."

General Douglas MacArthur, in a 1955 statement, is thought by some to have been involved with General George Marshall in establishing the Interplanetary Phenomenon Unit in 1947, supposedly formed to investigate UFO crashes; it is said to have been disbanded in the early 1950s. MacArthur's statement was:

> The nations of the world will have to unite, for the next war will be an interplanetary war. The nations of Earth must someday make a common front against attack by people from other planets.

Major Jesse Marcel, US Army Intelligence Officer in a videotaped interview, was noted as among the first to arrive at the crash site in Roswell. Marcel was well acquainted with all the weather balloons launched by the 509th Bomb Group, presumably including the Mogul balloons, one of which the US Government now claims accounts for the Roswell wreckage.

> I was amazed at what I saw. The amount of debris that was scattered over such an area.... The more I saw of the fragments, the more I realized it wasn't anything I was acquainted with. In fact, as it turned out, nobody else was acquainted with it.... There was a cover-up some place about this whole matter.

Others spoke out as well. Lt. Colonel James McAshan, USAF commented:

> In concealing the evidence of UFO operations, the Air Force is making a serious mistake.

Captain Eddie Rickenbacker, "American Ace of Aces," medal of honor-winning commander of the 94th Aero Pursuit Squadron in WWI, with twenty-six "kills" said:

> Flying saucers are real. Too many good men have seen them, that don't have hallucinations.

Colonel Carl Sanderson, USAF commenting on his sighting of two circular silver UFOs in close proximity to his plane over Hermanas, New Mexico:

> From their maneuvers and their terrific speed I am certain their flight performance was greater than any aircraft known today.

The UFOs were said to make a series of seemingly impossible maneuvers before disappearing at an astonishing speed and showing up again over El Paso, Texas.

Major Gerald Smith, USAF, one of the F-106 pilots who was scrambled under orders from NORAD (North American Air Defense Command) to investigate a UFO over West Palm Beach, Florida on September 14, 1972. The UFO was viewed through binoculars by the FAA supervisor, George Morales, sighted by an Eastern Airlines captain, police and several civilians, as well as being tracked on radar by Miami International Airport and Homestead AFB. The Major said:

> [There was] something definite in the sky.... If it had proved to be hostile we would have destroyed it.

Lieutenant D.A. Swimley, USAF, commented on a sighting of eight disc-shaped objects he and several fellow officers watched circling over Hamilton AFB, California, on August 3, 1953. The objects were also picked up on radar and spotted by many civilian pilots. F-86 Sabers were scrambled to intercept the objects, but the jets were apparently too slow. The Lieutenant said:

> And don't tell me they were reflections, I know they were solid objects.

Commanding General Nathan F. Twining of the Air Material Command, US A.A.F., in a declassified letter to the Pentagon reported:

> The phenomenon is something real and not visionary or fictitious. There are objects approximating the shape of a disc, some of which appear flat on bottom and domed on top. These objects are as large as man-made aircraft and have a metallic or light-reflecting surface. Further they exhibit extreme rates of climb and maneuverability with no associated sound and take action which must be considered evasive when contacted by aircraft and radar.

Colonel Robert Willingham, USAF, from an affidavit filed in the 1970s reported Willingham and his navigator were test flying an F-94 on Sept. 6, 1950 out of San Angelo, Texas when they were alerted by radar control operators of a UFO in their area.

Headquarters wouldn't let us go after it and we played around a little bit. We got to watching how it made 90 degree turns at this high speed and everything. We knew it wasn't a missile of any type. So then, we confirmed it with the radar control station, and they kept following it, and they claimed that it crashed somewhere off between Texas and the Mexico border.

Air Marshall Azim Daudpota, Zimbabwe, commented on a UFO witnessed in July of 1985 by many people and that was tracked on radar.

This was no ordinary UFO. Scores of people saw it. It was no illusion, no deception, no imagination.

Air Chief Marshall Lord Hugh Dowding, commanding officer of the Royal Air Force during WWII. The statement made in August of 1954 advised:

Of course UFOs are real – and they are interplanetary.... The cumulative evidence for the existence of UFOs is quite overwhelming and I accept the fact of their existence.

Colonel Fuijo Hayashi, Commander of the Air Transport Wing of Japan's Air Self-Defense Force made a statement sometime in the 1960s:

UFOs are impossible to deny.... It is very strange that we have never been able to find out the source for over two decades.

Lieutenant-General Akira Hirano, Chief of Staff of Japan's Air Self-Defense Force (ASDF), in September, 1977 said:

We frequently see unidentified objects in the sky. We are quietly investigating them.

General Kanshi Ishikawa, Chief of Air Staff of Japan's ASDF, in a statement in 1967, said:

UFOs are real and they may come from outer space...photographs and various materials show scientifically that there are more advanced people piloting the saucers and mother ships.

6

UFO Eyewitnesses
at Conference
in Washington, D.C.[17]

The following is the individual witness testimony distributed to those who attended the Briefing at the UFO Conference on Monday, September 26, 2010. This is in the order of the presentation speakers.

Speakers at the UFO Conference sponsored by the National Press Club, Washington, D.C.

Major General (Ret.) Wilfried De Brouwer, Belgian Air Force
Claude POHER, space research engineer (Ret.)
(Ret.) Air Force Captain Jean-Charles DUBOC

Jean-Claude Ribes, astronomer
General of the Iranian Air Force, Parviz Jafari (Ret.)
Rodrigo Bravo Garrido
Oscar Alfonso Santa Maria Huertas, (Ret.) Peruvian Air Force
Dr. Anthony Choy, founding member of the OIFAA
Nick Pope, formerly with the British Ministry of Defense
James Penniston (Ret.), United States Air Force
Charles I. Halt. (Ret.) Colonel US Air Force

Major General (Ret.) Wilfried De Brouwer

Retired Major General De Brouwer of the Belgian Air Force was Chief Operations officer when an exceptional UFO wave took place over Belgium. On the evening of 29 November 1989, in Eastern Belgium, approximately 140 UFO sightings were reported. What makes this case interesting is:

1. Hundreds of people saw a majestic triangular craft

2. The craft was a span of approximately 120 feet

3. There were powerful beaming spot lights

4. It was moving slowly (a speed at which most airplanes will stall)

5. It was not making any significant noise

6. In a few cases, it was accelerating to very high speeds

The UFO wave would last more than one year during which a Belgian UFO organization conducted the investigations consisting of:

1. More than 650 investigations

2. Recording more than 400 hours of audio witness reports

3. On one occasion, a photograph revealing the triangular shape and four light beams of the object

Note: Belgium had no official focal point for reporting UFO observations.

Major General De Brouwer stated:

> In my function of Chief Operations, I was confronted with numerous questions about the origin and nature of these craft. In the first instance, and in consultation with other NATO partners, I could confirm that no flights of stealth aircraft or any other experimental

aircraft look place in the airspace of Belgium. In addition, the Civil Aviation Authorities confirmed that no flight plans had been introduced. This implied that the reported object(s) committed an infraction against the existing aviation rules.

The Belgian Air Force, as would any country, tried to identify the alleged intruders over their air space. On one occasion, two F-16s registered rapid changes in speed and altitude which were well outside of the performance envelope of existing aircraft; the pilots could not establish visual contact in their investigation.

The technical evidence was insufficient to conclude that abnormal air activities took place during that evening.

Conclusion: In all the reports I have looked over and any information I could pull regarding these sightings I want to state that the Belgian UFO wave was exceptional and the Belgian Air Force could not identify the nature, origin and intentions of the reported phenomena.

Claude POHER

What makes Dr. Poher a person who would be creditable as a UFO witness?

1. He is a retired astrophysicist.

2. He worked as a space research engineer for the National Center for Space Studies.

3. He also was the founder of the GEPAN, the Group for the Study of Unidentified Aerospace Phenomena.

4. Dr. Poher began to investigate official French UFO reports, and to undertake scientific analyses of the data.

He trained his first investigators, teaching them how to conduct official investigations into the different kinds of reports, from lights in the sky to landings with physical evidence and observations of occupants. For example, he trained the investigators on the case of CUSSAC. This case happened:

1. August 1967.

2. Two young witnesses were alerted by the agitation of dozens of frightened farm animals at around noon.

3. They observed a landed spherical UFO at a distance of 80 yards.

4. The UFO held four occupants near the UFO, there size was 3 to 3 ½ feet tall.

Extremely high luminosity was reported after slow takeoff, leaving physiological effects on the eyes of the witness that were confirmed by the village mayor. A hissing noise was described by the two witnesses and was also heard by the hunting guard of the village.

Dr. Poher also stated that:

> The UFO acceleration after vertical takeoff was estimated to be about a hundred Gs by GEPAN experts. The occupants were seen floating in the air while entering the craft, from its top, in a hurry.

The physical traces on the ground from the craft were confirmed by the local police; it left a sulfur-oxide odor. The following agencies worked with the witnesses:

1. CNES experts in meteorology and space debris

2. A Judge

3. A psychologist

4. An optical engineer

5. An aeronautical engineer

According to GEPAN, the official conclusion in 1979 was that about fifteen percent of cases remained unidentified after careful analysis by experts. They concluded that the objects, in most of these cases, were compatible with flying machines whose flight physics were foreign to the expert's knowledge.

There were some more recent experimental facts, in direct relation to his GEPAN and UFO investigation involvement that he believes are of great importance for our future, and for the way we should now handle UFO observations in the USA.

Last April 2010, the physical theory about gravitation and inertia he was working on since the early 80s, was successfully tested in a laboratory. He has patented and tested devices and was able to reproduce the causes of the strange effects that are described in UFO observation reports. These effects include:

1. Tremendous accelerations

2. Sharp turns

3. Sudden stops

4. Powerful emission of light

5. Silent supersonic speed, etc.

The experimental results are currently open to be demonstrated in his laboratory in Toulouse, for scientists, scientific journalists, and industrial representatives, including those from the USA.

Jean-Charles DUBOC

Mr. Jean-Charles DUBOC is a retired Air France Captain. Mr. Duboc stated "that he and his crew observed a daylight UFO near Paris while he was piloting Air France flight 3532." Important information in these sightings are:

1. Date: January 28, 1994

2. Time: 13:00 hours (1:30 p.m.)

3. Three witnesses:
   • Pilot
   • Co-pilot
   • Steward

4. Visibility was excellent with some altocumulus clouds

The object had been identified initially by a steward as a weather balloon, but when Capt. DUBOC identified it, it looked quite different.

Note: All three witnesses were in the cockpit. The UFO was in evolution and it looked like a huge flying disk. It then banked at a 45° angle. It stabilized and stopped moving.

Capt. DUBOC also stated that:

We observed it (the UFO) for over one minute on the LEFT of our plane; surprisingly, it seemed totally stationary in the sky, and it disappeared progressively. This large object was below us at the altitude of 35,000 feet. We were at 39,000 feet at a distance of about 25 nautical miles.

Description of the UFO craft:

1. The color was RED BROWN with BLURRED outlines.

2. The diameter of the object was the diameter of the moon or sun. (That would mean it was about 1000 feet wide.)

3. We had no idea of the structure of the UFO

4. It seemed to be embedded in a kind of magnetic or gravitational field.

5. There were no lights.

6. There was no visual metallic structure (which gave it a really FUZZY appearance).

7. It became transparent and disappeared in about 10 to 20 seconds.

8. The three witnesses quickly realized that what they were seeing did not resemble anything known to them.

9. It was reported to Reims traffic control.

10. The radar of the Operational Centre of the Air Defense (the CODA), registered a one minute spot crossing the track of our plane.

11. It was near the base of Tavemy (which hosts the headquarters of the French Strategic Air Command).

This sighting has been studied by the French military COMETA group, several high ranking officers of the French Defense, and by GEPAN under the French National Space Centre (CNES).

Conclusion: The investigation determined this could not have been a weather balloon, and estimated the approximate length of the UFO to have been 800 feet. This sighting remains unexplained.

Jean-Claude Ribes

Jean-Claude Ribes is a good witness to UFO investigators because:

1. He is an astronomer,

2. He worked for the French National Center for Scientific Research from 1963 to 1998.

3. He contributed to the French COMETA report, a three year military study on UFOs and National Security released in 1999.

Mr. Ribes stated:

> Last March, 2010, my country took a big step forward. GEIPAN released the French UFO files to the public.

The files were posted on a website detailing:

1. More than 1,600 sightings spanning five decades.

2. Some of these cases involved multiple sightings and physical evidence such as bum marks and radar trackings.

3. Others documented UFOs with flight patterns or accelerations defying the laws of physics.

Unfortunately, they do not have any proof at all that extra-terrestrials are behind the unexplained phenomena; on the flip side, they do have proof that they aren't.

Ribes' personal opinion is that UFOs should be taken seriously and studied without prejudice. There could be several possible explanations, such as:

1. Rare atmospheric phenomena,

2. Some cases strongly suggest actual flying machines with characteristics well beyond our terrestrial capacities. If these cases could be completely proven as such, then the extraterrestrial hypothesis would probably be the most likely explanation for these advanced craft.

Parviz Jafari

This case is an exciting case both for ufology and the military around the world.

General Parviz Jafari, is a retired General of Iranian Air Force, who stated:

> On the evening of September 18, 1976, at about 2300 hours (11 p.m.), citizens were frightened by the circling of an unknown object over Tehran, the Capital city of Iran, at a low altitude.

Details:

1. It looked similar to a star, but bigger and brighter.

2. It was seen by the air control tower.

3. The tower alerted the Air Force command post.

4. Deputy General Yousefi decided to scramble an F-4 jet to investigate.

After launching the F-4 fighters, several things seemed to happen all at one:

1. The pilot in the first jet lost instrumentation.

2. The pilot lost all communications when he got too close to the brilliant object, so he headed back.

3. About 10 minutes later, the Air Force scrambled a second jet.

4. The object was flashing with intense red, green, orange, and blue light so bright that the pilot was not able to see its body.

5. The sequence of flashes was extremely fast, like a strobe light.

6. Lieutenant Jafari locked on the UFO with radar:
   • It was at 30° left,
   • At a range of 25 miles.

7. The size on the radar scope was comparable to that of a 707 commercial passenger jet.

When Lieutenant Jafari tried to lock on to the UFO, four objects with different shapes separated from the main craft, at different times, during this close encounter. Every time the UFO came close to him, his weapons jammed and his radio communications were garbled.

One of the objects headed toward him and Lieutenant Jafari thought it was a missile. He immediately tried to launch a heat-seeking missile to counteract it, but the missile panel went out (malfunction). He stated that he tried to return to the base and another object followed him. One of the separated objects landed in an open area radiating a high bright light, so bright that the sand on the ground was visible.

It was also reported by other airliners flying at the time and continued for another couple of days. During an interview, an American colonel took notes, but after it was over, Lieutenant Jafari could not find him to talk to.

Conclusion: Lieutenant Jafari and the other pilots who reported this sighting gave us great detail on the description and actions of the UFO and the orbs that came from the craft. The Defense Intelligence Agency was very interested in this sighting and documented the event in great detail; the report was then sent to NSA, The White House, and the CIA. The DIA assessment of this case:

- It is a classic.

- It meets all necessary conditions for a legitimate study of the UFO phenomenon.

Remember, this is 1976, possibly into 1977; the United States Government (particularly the US Air Force) quit investigating UFOs and stated that UFOs did not pose any threat to national security. Having the technology to jam communications, jam weapons panels, and being able to move around at high speeds, with nothing the military can do about it, IS A THREAT TO NATIONAL SECURITY.

Rodrigo Bravo Garrido

Chile is located in South America and is one of the most stable and prosperous nations. It has been relatively free of the coups and arbitrary governments that have blighted the continent.

Since the beginning of Chilean history, there have been hundreds of reports of unidentified phenomena, sometimes called UFOs, observed in their skies. In October of 1997, the Department of Civil Aeronautics, (the Chilean equivalent of the American FAA), set up the Committee for the Study of Anomalous Aerial Phenomena, known as the CEFAA. This agency handles the best reports of unidentified aerial phenomena in cooperation with aeronautic specialists.

One of the most important civil aviation cases occurred in 1988. A Boeing 737 pilot was on final approach to the runway at the Tepual Airport in Puerto Montt City, when it suddenly encountered a large white light surrounded by green and red. This light was moving in the opposite direction of the aircraft, coming straight at it. The pilot had to make a steep turn to the left in order to avoid a collision. The phenomenon was observed by the control tower personnel.

Note: Federal agencies state that our skies are safe; I believe this shows us that unidentified flying objects can be a danger for air operations and are a danger to any plane or craft flying in our skies. Here again, we have a pilot witnessing the event and air traffic control also monitoring the event. What will it take for the governments around the world to change their way of thinking and finally admit the existence of UFOs/UAPs?

Another case in 2000 involved the crew of a Chilean plane (Aviation branch of the Army) flying South of Santiago. They observed a long cigar-shaped object; the color was a brilliant gray. It flew parallel to the right side of the aircraft for two minutes and then disappeared. This object was detected by the radar of the Control Center of Santiago which notified the crew minutes before the incident.

Mr. Garrido stated that:

> New cases are being documented by pilots, traffic controllers, operations staff at the world's airports, and by many others with the proper training to determine if a flying object is something unusual. The true origin of these UFOs is unknown, yet they do affect aviation all around the planet, and this must be addressed.

Conclusion: I am happy to say that NARCAP has signed an agreement with the UAP research team of Chile, CEFAA – The Committee for the Study of Anomalous Aerial Phenomena – in mid December 2010. Both of these organizations have recognized that we share common observations and concerns and that a formal research pact could be mutually beneficial. It is a small step, but at least governments are trying to work together to find some kind of answers.

Oscar Alfonso Santa Maria Huertas (See Chapter 2)

This UFO case is extremely exciting for UFO enthusiasts; it also has been debunked over the years. As an investigator, I find this case important for several reasons.

1. The witness is Oscar Santa Maria Huertas, retired pilot of the Peruvian Air Force.

2. This case was witnessed by over 1,800 men and women stationed at a military installation. [1,600 in some accounts.]

3. The UFO changes shapes.

4. A professional military pilot with years of experienced fired upon the UFO with NO EFFECT.

5. The UFO had the capability to change the course of bullets traveling at a rate of 2,880 feet per second.

6. The bullets that did hit the target, caused no damage; they were absorbed into the craft.

The following is Oscar Alfonso Santa Maria Huertas statement of events:

> On the morning of April 11, 1980, at 7:15, 1,800 men were in formation at the Air Base of La Joya, Arequipa. They all observed a stationary object in the sky:

- Which looked like a balloon,

- At about three miles distance, and

- Approximately 1,800 feet altitude.

- It reflected the sun.

My unit commander ordered me to take off in my Sukosi-22 jet and shoot down the spherical object. It was in restricted airspace, without clearance, and we were concerned about espionage. I approached the object and fired sixty-four 30mm shells at it. Some projectiles went towards the ground, and others hit the object fully, but they had no effect at all.

Note: The wall of fire that a 30mm x 165 sends out would normally obliterate anything in its path. The rate of fire is so quick it can hit a quarter twice inside an inch.

Other important facts of this case are:

1. The object then began to ascend, and move farther away from the base.

2. It made a sudden stop, forcing the pilot to veer to the side. (He was only 1,500 feet away.)

3. Just as he had locked onto the target and was ready to shoot, the object made a straight vertical climb evading the attack.

4. Two other times he had the object on target, when the object was stationary. Every time, it moved away at the very last minute, when the pilot was just about to fire, always eluding his attack.

5. It began to ascend almost parallel to his plane, at an altitude of 63,000 feet; it stopped. [62,000 feet in some reports]

6. The UFO was about 30 feet in diameter.

7. It was an enameled, cream-colored dome, with a wide, circular, metallic base.

8. It had no engines, no exhausts, no windows, no wings, or antennae.

9. It lacked all the typical aircraft components, with no visible propulsion system.

It was at that moment Huertas realized it was a UFO, something totally unknown. He was almost out of fuel and afraid. He radioed for another plane to come and have a look, trying to hide his fear. They said no, and ordered him back. After he landed, the object remained stationary in the sky for two hours, for everyone at the base to see. A US Department of Defense document titled "UFO Sighted in Peru" described the incident, stating that the vehicle's origin remains unknown.

Conclusion: This case is one of those that there are no answers; is it a real UFO, or was it a secret air-craft that happened to be seen by thousands of witnesses? How do you explain bullets having no impact on the craft? If this is a real UFO, could we ever defend ourselves if they decided to attack? Seems to be more questions than answers, but what the response of the military to these UFO activities will be? Governments are not talking.

Dr. Anthony Choy

Dr. Anthony Choy is a founding member of the OIFAA which was established by the Peruvian Air Force in December, 2001. He is also the author of Project 33, the first integral study on the UFO phenomenon in Peru.

One of the cases Dr. Choy talks about took place in the northern city of Chulucanas on October 13, 2001. The facts in the case are:

1. Hundreds of people got to see eight spheres of light

2. They were an intense red-orange color

3. The spheres were recorded on video

4. These objects were suspended in the air for over five hours

5. They were moving in an apparently intelligent manner

6. They traveled in absolute silence

7. Then they disappeared

A few days later, on October 25th, a luminous tear-shaped object of some 82 feet in diameter (approximately 25 meters), was recorded over the countryside near the city; a few minutes later, an apparent landing of light spheres in the woods was also recorded.

In February of 2002, the Air Force's FAA ordered Dr. Choy to investigate these sightings. In February 2003, Peruvian Air Force Colonel Jose Raffo Moloche, Director of Aerial and Space Concerns, made an open statement to the media acknowledging that the Chulucanas Incident was the first official UFO investigation in Peru.

The conclusion of these cases are, although being physically real, they had no explanation. The case remains open, and the investigation continues independently. On August 6 of 2004, the American television channel of Univision was able to record for fifty-five minutes a distant object of unknown nature and origin, moving at great velocity in the sky, going up and down, and right and left.

Note: I would like to add that the Air Force has taken the right steps by opening an office to conduct these investigations – actual UFO cases and incidents that have taken place in all countries; and this shows that the UFO phenomenon remains one of the greatest challenges to our current knowledge of science and technology. More countries should follow the Peruvian government and start taking the UFO Phenomenon seriously, and be open to the people of the world and talk about the subject openly.

Nick Pope

Nick Pope was formerly with the British Ministry of Defense. The British Government has received over 10,000 UFO reports since 1950. The responsibility for this subject rests with the Ministry of Defense, and Nick Pope's job was to look for evidence of any potential threat to the UK. Mr. Pope had this job from 1991-1994.

As with most countries, a majority of these UFO sightings turned out to be misidentifications of things such as:

- Aircraft
- Satellites
- Meteors

Mr. Pope stated that:

> ...around five percent of cases, no explanation could be found. These cases include incidents where reliable witnesses, such as police officers and pilots, reported structured craft performing speeds and maneuvers significantly in excess of anything they had seen military jet aircraft perform. Other cases included in this category involved UFOs tracked on radar and incidents where photos or videos were produced and where the MoD's technical experts found no evidence of fakery.

In March 1993, Mr. Pope investigated a case where a UFO was seen by about sixty witnesses, including military personnel at two air force bases. Witnesses included a patrol officer of air force police, together with a meteorological officer with 8 years experience. The meteorological officer described:

1. A triangular-shaped craft midway in size between a C-130 and a Boeing 747.

2. It was emitting a low frequency humming sound,

3. It moved slowly at first, before accelerating away many times faster than a military jet.

Mr. Pope added,

> My Assistant Chief of the Air Staff concluded in summary, there would seem to be some evidence on this occasion that an unidentified object (or objects) of unknown origin was operating over the UK.

The case file – published on the MoD website – also mentions related inquiries from the US authorities, asking if the UK had a black program that might explain some UFO sightings involving large triangular-shaped craft. That's interesting, given the US government's public position that UFOs are no longer investigated.

James Penniston

James Penniston has been witness to one of the best UFO observations since the Betty and Barny Hill abduction case in the 60s. His observations of this case was a big help to the UFO world of believers. I am talking about the Rendlesham Forest sighting on the 26th of December 1980.
James Penniston was:

- A sergeant, United States Air Force, Retired.

- Assigned to the largest Tactical Fighter Wing in the Air Force, RAF Woodbridge in England.

- Was the senior security officer in charge of base security

- At that time, held a top-secret US and NATO security clearance.

- Was responsible for the protection of war-making resources. for that base

Mr. Penniston stated:

> Shortly after midnight on the 26th of December, 1980, Staff Sergeant Steffens briefed me that some lights were seen in Rendlesham Forest, just outside the base. He informed me that whatever it was didn't crash.... It landed.

Unfortunately, he discounted what Staff Sergeant Steffens said and reported to the control center back at the base that they had a possible report of a downed aircraft. He then ordered Airman Cabanzak and A1C Burroughs to respond with him.

Mr. Penniston states:

> When we arrived near the suspected crash site, it quickly became apparent that we were not dealing with a plane crash or anything else we had ever responded to.

Here is what they saw:

1. There was a bright light emanating from an object on the forest floor.

2. It appeared as a silhouetted, triangular craft.

3. It measured approximately 9 feet long by 6.5 feet high.

4. The craft was fully intact.

5. It was sitting in a small clearing inside the woods.

6. They started experiencing problems with their radios.

7. As they approached the triangular-shaped craft, there were blue and yellow lights swirling around the exterior as though part of the surface.

8. They noticed the air around them was electrically charged.

9. They could feel the charges on their cloths, skin, and hair.

As most close encounter witnesses have stated, nothing in their training prepared them for what they were witnessing. Following security protocol, they completed a thorough on-site investigation, and this included a full physical examination of the craft, photographs, notebook entries, and radio relays through airman Cabansag to the control center as required. On one side of the craft they noticed there were symbols that measured about three inches high and two and a half feet across. The symbols they saw were:

- Pictorial in design.

- The largest symbol was a triangle, located in the center of the others.

- Those symbols were etched into the surface of the craft.

- The craft was warm to the touch and felt like metal.

Sergeant Penniston said on several occasions during interviews that, "The feeling I had during this encounter was no type of aircraft that I've ever seen before." Sergeant Penniston states:

> After roughly forty-five minutes, the light from the craft began to intensify. Burroughs and I then took a defensive position away from the craft as it lifted off the ground without any noise or air disturbance. It maneuvered through the trees and shot off at an unbelievable rate of speed. It was gone in the blink of an eye.

Conclusion: The Air Force stated that the information acquired during the investigation was reported through proper military channels. The investigating team and witnesses were told to treat the investigation as top secret and no further discussion was allowed. The photos that were retrieved from the base lab (two rolls of 35 mm) were apparently over exposed. In some reports, you notice the Air Force states they never had any photos.

Note: As an investigator, this is frustrating. Here is a case where the witnesses were able to walk up to the craft, take notes, inform supervisors of the symbols on the craft. But all the people are told is: "It is a top secret case and no further discussion is allowed."

Charles I. Halt

Charles I. Halt is a retired Colonel from the US Air Force. Mr. Halt experience goes a long way – he was:

1. A base commander at two large installations,

2. The Director, Inspections Directorate for the DOD 1G, and

3. His responsibility included inspection oversight of all military services and defense agencies.

This case coincides with Sergeant Penniston from the case listed prior. In 1980, Charles I. Halt was the Deputy Base Commander of RAF Bentwaters, which consisted of a twin-base complex in East Anglia, England. This base was the largest Tactical Fighter Wing in the Air Force.

Colonel Halt was called to investigate an event that was distracting Base Security Police from their primary duties. The Base Security Police discovered strange lights in the forest east of the back gate of RAE Woodbridge. Three patrolmen were dispatched into the forest to investigate. They reported:

1. A strange triangular craft sitting on three legs,

2. The craft was approximately 10 feet (3 meters) on each side.

3. The craft had multiple lights.

4. It rapidly maneuvered and quickly left the area.

Colonel Halt stated that he:

> ...was not immediately aware of the details, only being told of strange lights and assumed there was a reasonable explanation. Two nights later, the family Christmas party was interrupted by the on-duty police commander. He told of strange events and claimed it was back. Since my boss had to present awards, I was tasked to go out and investigate. I fully expected to find an explanation.

Colonel Halt took four other military personnel with him to investigate the lights. He took:

1. Two senior Security Police,

2. A Disaster Preparedness expert, and

3. The reporting On Duty Police Commander.

At the site, they found the three indentations in the ground in a triangular pattern. The Disaster Preparedness Officer who went with Halt had a Geiger counter, and he started taking readings. The Geiger counter indicated a small amount of radiation, nothing serious, and evidence including broken branches.

They suddenly observed a bright red/orange oval object with a black center. It maneuvered horizontally through the trees with occasionally vertical movement. When they approached the light, it receded and silently broke into five white lights which quickly vanished. When they left the forest and went into a pasture they observed several objects with multiple lights in the Northern sky. They changed in shape from elliptical to round. Colonel Halt said:

> Several other objects were seen to the South. One approached at high speed and sent down a concentrated beam near our feet. Another object sent down beams into the weapons storage area. The whole time we had difficulty communicating with the base as all three radio frequencies kept breaking up. This activity continued for about an hour. During this entire event, I had my pocket recorder and taped the event as it unfolded. A copy of the tape was released without my knowledge. I have no idea what we saw, but do know whatever we saw, was under intelligent control.

Multiple Sightings
Over Belgium

 On March 30 and 31, 1990, the UFO sightings in Belgian peaked, on those nights:

Unknown objects were tracked on radar, and were seen by more than 13,500 witnesses on the ground, and were photographed.

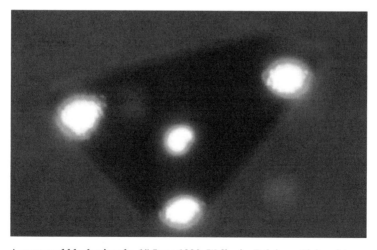

A supposed black triangle, 15 June 1990, Wallonia, Belgium. Claimed to have been taken during the UFO wave, though released thirteen years later in Wallonia, Belgium, Europe. Bear in mind that there has never been a clear picture of a true UFO, so the resolution is not the best. (From the original photograph collection: *The photographer hereby releases these photographs into the public domain. All claims to copyrights have been surrendered. Pictures taken 15 June 1990 Wallonia Belgium by J.S. Henrardi*)

Of the witnesses stated above, more than 2,600 reported written statements describing in detail the events they saw. The following report of the incident is from the Belgian air force detailing the events of that night.

At around 23:00 [11 p.m.] on 30 March the supervisor for the Control Reporting Center (CRC) at Glons received reports that three unusual lights were seen moving towards Thorembais-Gembloux which lies to the South-East of Brussels (from Gembloux is 11.25 miles at 337.15 degrees).

The lights were reported to be brighter than stars, changing colors between red, green, and yellow, and appeared to be fixed at the vertices of an equilateral triangle. At this point, Glons CRC requested the Wavre gendarmerie send a patrol to confirm the sighting. (Wavre is just west of Brussels)

Approximately ten minutes later, a second set of lights was sighted moving towards the first triangle. By around 23:30 [11:30 p.m.], the Wavre gendarmerie had confirmed the initial sightings and Glons CRC had been able to observe the phenomenon on radar. During this time, the second set of lights, after some erratic maneuvers, had also formed themselves into a smaller triangle. After tracking the targets and after receiving a second radar confirmation from the Traffic Center Control at Semmerzake, Glons, CRC gave the order to scramble two F-16 fighters from Beauvechain Air Base shortly before midnight. Throughout this time, the phenomenon was still clearly visible from the ground, with witnesses describing the whole formation as maintaining their relative positions while moving slowly across the sky. Witnesses also reported two dimmer lights towards the municipality of Eghezee displaying similar erratic movements to the second set of lights.-

Belgium F-16s sitting on deck ready to scramble.

Over the next hour, the two scrambled F-16s attempted nine separate interceptions of the targets. On three occasions, they managed to obtain a radar lock for a few seconds, but each time, the targets changed position and sped so rapidly that the lock was broken. During the first radar lock, the target accelerated from 240 km/h (149 mph) to over 1,770 km/h (1,100 mph) while changing altitude from 2,700 m (8,775 feet) to 1,500 m (4,875 feet), then up to 3,350 m (10,887.5 feet) before descending to almost ground level – the first descent of more than 900 m (2,700 feet) taking less than two seconds. Similar maneuvers were observed during both subsequent radar locks. On no occasion were the F-16 pilots able to make visual contact with the targets and at no point, despite the speeds involved, was there any indication of a sonic boom. Moreover, narrator Robert Stack added in an episode of *Unsolved Mysteries*,

> The sudden changes in acceleration and deceleration would have been fatal to one or more human pilots.

During this time, ground witnesses broadly corroborate the information obtained by radar. They described seeing the smaller triangle completely disappear from sight at one point, while the larger triangle moved upwards very rapidly as the F-16s flew past. After 00:30 [12:30 a.m.] radar contact became much more sporadic and the final confirmed lock took place at 00:40. [12:40 a.m.] This final lock was once again broken by an acceleration from around 100 mph to 695 mph (160 km/h to 1,120 km/h) after which the radar of the F-16s and those at Glons and Semmerzake all lost contact. Following several further unconfirmed contacts the F-16s eventually returned to base shortly after 01:00 [1 a.m.].

The final details of the sighting were provided by the members of the Wavre gendarmerie who had been sent to confirm the original report. They describe four lights being arranged in a square formation, all making short jerky movements, before gradually losing their luminosity and disappearing in four separate directions at around 01:30 [1:30 a.m.].

8

UFO Over Paris^{29, 30}

A Captain on an A320 Airbus observed a UFO. (Pilots are one of our best sources for Unidentified Aerial Phenomenon; they are in our skies on a regular basis, they know what other planes and aerial crafts look like.)

First of all, not only did the captain see this craft, but also the co-pilot and the steward, who both were in the cockpit. This case has been confirmed by a RADAR ECHO, recorded at the Center for Operations of Aerial Defence.

This sighting is now quite popular within the ufology community, and more recently, it has reached a vast audience through various TV shows.

The three witnesses were on board flight AF 3532, from Nice to London, on an A320 Airbus, on January 28th, 1994. The time was 01:14 p.m. They were cruising at an altitude of 39,000 feet, at some 12 miles North-West of the beacon of Coulommiers. The weather conditions were excellent. Then the steward pointed out to an object which he thought could be a weather balloon.

The co-pilot did confirm right away the sighting, and she, as well, thought of a weather balloon. Then the captain said that it could be an airplane, banking with a 45° gradient, which did not make any sense at this altitude.

Very quickly they had to realize that their sighting would not match with any known object, and that they were dealing with a UFO. Thanks to a one hundred percent clear sky, and considering there were some Altocumulus (culminating somewhere between 16,500 feet and 23,000 feet), the pilot has been able to estimate that this UFO was cruising at an altitude of 35,000 feet, and its distance to them was approximately 25 nautical miles.

It is important to mention that when you fly a commercial airplane traveling at a speed of over 200 meters/second, it is pretty easy to evaluate how far another airplane would be, judging by the time it takes to slide by your side.

Considering its visible diameter, and that of the moon, meaning 1/4 of the thickness of your forefinger with your arm straight, or 30 degrees, they figured out that the object was a huge one, because a standard airplane would not be visible at such a remote distance.

Its shape was that of a gigantic dark red lentil evolving, with blurred outlines, and they were able to stare at it for over a minute, on their left side. The most amazing part is that this craft disappeared gradually, within ten or fifteen seconds, as if it had dematerialized.

Accordingly, with the flight regulations, they were required to report the sighting to the air traffic control, located in Reims. They did, and Air Traffic Control replied that they had no information whatsoever on any other flight around them.

With the current process, the Reims air traffic control informed the CODA (Center for Operations of the Aerial Defence), located in Taverny.

Once back at Charles de Gaulle Airport, the chief A320 pilot asked the pilot of the flight to write a report, but he discarded his demand because the characteristics of this UFO were far beyond the pilot's scientific knowledge, and the main reason was that he had never been briefed on this type of phenomenon.

Only three years later, in 1997, the pilot was reading an article in *Paris-Match* magazine, and he learned that the Center for Operations of the Aerial Defence had taped, at the exact same timing, a radar track initiated by the monitoring center of Cinq-Mars-la-Pile. It was precisely, identical time and location, the very same sighting.

So he, the pilot, decided, because this Radar Identification did exist, to file a report with the Gendarmerie Nationale at Charles de Gaulle Airport, which consequently processed it to the Sepra (CNES). This report was forwarded to the study group for UFOs, established within the Institute of Advanced Studies for National Defense.

When the pilot was called for a meeting with the study group (The COMETA), that was held at the Military School in March 1997, they did confirm that a radar track of the UFO had been taped and it lasted for 50 seconds. The object had cruised short of one nautical mile (1,852 m) from flight AF 3532. On top of that, the phenomenon had vanished at the very same time, from their sight and the radar scopes.

The investigations conducted by the CODA had rejected the weather balloon hypothesis, and now they had a precise evaluation of the distance where the two radar beams had crossed.

During this same meeting, the size of the UFO had been estimated to be around 800 feet long, but this is a rough appreciation, and today the pilot would rather say 1,300 feet long (with an error margin of + or

- 300 feet), accordingly with a visible angle of 30 degrees, and a distance of 25 NM.

Let's add that the Regional Air Traffic Centre, which monitors traffic of at least 3,000 flights each day, has only examined three cases in the last seven years, among them flight AF 3532.

When you read this case in the COMETA report, it is not easy to understand that the radar identification and their visual observation from within the cockpit are not coincidental, but that is what truly happened.

The thing is, while they were staring at the object, THE UFO WAS ON THEIR LEFT SIDE, some 25 nautical miles away (47 km), but the RADAR TRACK goes from right to left, and crosses their path within ONE NAUTICAL MILE (1.8 km).

The visual sighting can be summed up as follows:

1. Visible Angle: that of the Moon, or 1/4 of the thickness of one forefinger (arm straight), or else 0°30'.

2. Distance: 25 nautical miles.

3. Lentil shape

4. Colour: dark red

5. Blur outlines

6. Showed a 45-bank angle on first sight

7. Sighting time lapse: 1-2mn

The radar monitoring can be summed up as follows:

1. Echo lasted for: 50 seconds

2. Heading 240 (West)

3. Estimated speed: 100 knots

The timings seem to match; also, the radar identification and the sighting are simultaneous. Indeed, the radar track crosses the Airbus path within one nautical mile, while we saw that this UFO remained still, at a range of about 25 nautical miles, on the left side.

Could there be a total inconsistency between the sighting and the radar identification? With such a case, it is well possible to build various hypothesis, which all could be, more or less, within the realm of science-fiction, and this one would be relevant to it!

The witnesses feel that this UFO was real, and it has generated some kind of an artificial radar echo, far away from its location, through an electronic counter-measures system, in order to avoid any risk of being attacked by the world's Aerial Forces. Think of the domain of electronic war-games that our children like to play, and your opponent is distracted towards a lure. Had a missile been fired, aimed at the UFO, the A320 Airbus would probably have been hit!

The pilot has ideas concerning the origin of this spaceship – because he thinks we are dealing with a spaceship. He has listed 4 hypotheses:

- **The first hypothesis:** This sighting may have been a DEMO OF THEIR POWER AND TECHNOLOGICAL ABILITIES by an ALIEN civilization which is willing to show up, officially, in broad daylight, over a major city.

- **The second hypothesis:** The seen object is an AMERICAN CRAFT. Indeed, the crash retrieval of a UFO in Roswell is now considered as fact, and American forces may have achieved some important technological leaps.

- **The third hypothesis:** This demonstration of such a technological power is due to an ALIEN CIVILIZATION, TEAMING WITH THE AMERICANS. This hypothesis is relatively tough; it would mean cooperation between Extra Terrestrials and the United States in the field of space technology.

- **The fourth hypothesis:** This object is neither terrestrial, nor extraterrestrial, but something else. Among the different possibilities, that of a terrestrial object visiting from our FUTURE.

9

UFO Phenomenon by GEPAN [31,32]

Taking into account the facts that we have gathered from the observers and from the location of their observations, we concluded that there generally can be said to be a material phenomenon behind the observations. In sixty percent of the cases reported here, the description of this phenomenon is apparently one of a flying machine whose origin, modes of lifting and/or propulsion are totally outside our knowledge.

~GEPAN Report to the Scientific Committee,
June, 1978

Dr. Claude Poher, Ph.D. in astronomy,
founder and first director of GEPAN,
the UFO investigative office under the French government's
National Center for Space Sciences which analyzed reports
from the Gendarmerie from 1974 through 1978,
writing in the GEPAN Report to the Scientific Committee,
June, 1978, Vol. 1, Chapter 4.

For more than 20 years, the French space agency has conducted a non-military but official investigation into UFO reports. In its first phase, the project was named GEPAN and its focus was primarily on UFO reports. Subsequently, the project was renamed SEPRA and was assigned a more general responsibility for studying all atmospheric reentry phenomena. In the body of the report, we have for convenience referred to the project as "GEPAN/SEPRA." This appendix gives a brief summary of the history, mission, operations and achievements of this project.

The French space agency is known as CNES (Centre National d'Études Spatiales). It was founded in 1962 to conduct French space activities on a national basis and also in the context of the European Space Agency (ESA) or of other international collaborations. CNES currently has 2,500 employees. The CNES headquarters are in Paris, but its technical center is in Toulouse.

GEPAN (Groupe d'Études des Phénomènes Aérospatiaux Non-identifiés) – Study Group for Unidentified Aerospace Phenomena – was established as a department of CNES in Toulouse in 1977. At that time, its head was Dr. Claude Poher, who had already performed statistical analyses of files containing several thousand observations worldwide (Poher, 1973). CNES set up a scientific advisory board comprising astronomers, physicists, legal experts and other eminent citizens to monitor and guide GEPAN's activities.

The first tasks undertaken by GEPAN were:

- To establish data collection procedures in conjunction with the Air Force, civil aviation authorities, the Gendarmerie (French internal police), meteorological offices, the national police, etc.
- To conduct statistical analyses of eye-witness reports.
- To investigate previously reported cases.

These initial studies led to the following conclusions:

- Those events that remain unexplained after careful analysis are neither numerous nor frequent.
- The appearance of some reported phenomena cannot readily be interpreted in terms of conventional physical, psychological, or psycho-social models.
- The existence of a physical component of these phenomena seems highly likely.

Following these initial steps, GEPAN undertook to develop a more theoretical but rigorous approach to these studies. It was clear at the outset that it would be necessary to consider both the physical nature and the psychological nature of the phenomenon. In order to fully understand a witness's narrative account, it was necessary to consider not only the account but the psychology and personality of the witness, the physical environment in which the event occurred, and the witness's psycho-social environment.

GEPAN negotiated agreements with the Gendarmerie Nationale, the Air Force, the Navy, the meteorological offices, police, etc. These negotiations led to procedures by which these organizations provided GEPAN with relevant reports, video tapes, films, etc., which were then processed and analyzed either by GEPAN or by associated laboratories. However, from 1979 on, GEPAN worked mainly with reports from the Gendarmerie since these reports proved to be best suited for GEPAN's purposes.

GEPAN developed a classification system to reflect the level of difficulty in understanding the reports:

Type A: The phenomenon is fully and unambiguously identified.

Type B: The nature of the phenomenon has probably been identified but some doubt remains.

Type C: The report cannot be analyzed since it lacks precision, so no opinion can be formed.

Type D: The witness testimony is consistent and accurate but cannot be interpreted in terms of conventional phenomena.

Reports of Type A and Type B were further subdivided into astronomical, aeronautical, space, miscellaneous, and identified. GEPAN carried out statistical analyses aimed at classifying cases according to sets of physical characteristics.

Two types of investigations were carried out on individual reports: Mini-investigations, that were applied to cases of limited significance; and Full investigations, that were applied to unexplained cases (Type D) in which effort was made to obtain as much information as possible, including gathering and analyzing physical and biological evidence.

During the GEPAN phase, the project initiated several lines of research involving other laboratories and consultants. These were aimed at seeking a possible basis for modeling unexplained aspects of UFO reports, as well as seeking new techniques for the more active investigation of UFO events by the development of detection systems. These research topics included the following.

Research on possible magneto hydrodynamic propulsion systems

Study of facilities to collect unexpected atmospheric phenomena on a worldwide basis, that led to the proposal of the Eurociel Project to develop a network of ground stations equipped with wide-angle observation systems and powerful real-time processing algorithms; methodology for image analysis (photographs, videos, etc.); and study of aeronautical cases, especially radar-visual cases.

In 1988, GEPAN was replaced by SEPRA (Service d'Expertise des Phénomènes de Rentrées Atmosphériques – Atmospheric Re-entry Phenomena Expertise Department). M. J-J. Velasco, who had been a member of GEPAN since the very beginning, took charge of this new project that was then assigned a wider mission. This new project was called upon to investigate all re-entry phenomena including debris from satellites, launches, etc. However, the budget was drastically reduced so that research into UFO reports could not be maintained at the earlier level. Nevertheless, all existing official procedures concerning data collection have been maintained to ensure continuity in receiving reports.

After 21 years of activity, the GEPAN/SEPRA files now contain about 3,000 UFO reports supplied by the Gendarmerie. About 100 of these reports were found to justify specific investigations. Of this number, only a few cases remain unexplained today.

There have been attempts by SEPRA to increase the scope of the project at least to a European level, but this has not yet been successful. One of these attempts was the "Eurociel" project: The basic concept was to implement two sets of wide-angle optical detection stations, sited some tens of miles apart following a parallel of latitude, each station to be equipped with CCD-type cameras, with a minimum of one in the visible and one in the infrared. The output from these cameras would feed data into a microcomputer that triggers recording of the data when the computer determines that a change has suddenly occurred. The data from all these stations would be stored in a central facility to permit the calculation of trajectories. Such a system could detect lightning, meteors, unknown satellites, and other known or unknown phenomena.

During the GEPAN phase, the project produced many reports and investigations and technical documents concerning topics related to the study of UFO events. These reports were made publicly available. These reports are no longer being disseminated, but some information can still be requested from CNES.

10

Rendlesham Forest As Seen by Sgt. James Penniston[40, 41]

Thirty one years ago on December 26, 1980, US Air Force Staff Sergeant James Penniston was stationed in the 81st Security Police Squadron at the large joint British and US Air Force base known as RAF (Royal Air Force) Bentwaters and its smaller, secondary base at Woodbridge, about three miles away, where some aircraft were kept. Shortly after midnight on December 26, Sgt. Penniston was asked to investigate odd lights seen moving in the Rendlesham Forest between Bentwaters and Woodbridge. Joining him was USAF Airman First Class John Burroughs and several other security and military personnel.

As the men approached the odd lights about 984 feet (300 meters) off the main access road in the trees, the men could see blue, yellow, red, and white colors were pulsing.

What the men saw, none of them will every forget:

1. Triangular craft.

2. The size of the craft was 9 feet long.

3. It was 7 to 8 feet high [some reports say 6.5 feet and 10 feet].

4. It was black, smooth, like glass

5. The underside had a bluish/white glow.

6. It had a blinking red light on top of the craft.

7. There was no sound.

8. A high electrical static in the air.

9. You could feel the static on your skin and hair.

10. Movement didn't feel "normal," it was as if a person was moving in slow motion.

11. Next day, Penniston went back to the site and discovered triangular (2.5m apart) landing indentations on the ground where the UFO was, and made plaster casts.

Sgt. James Penniston stated:

> Well, I couldn't tell at that point, but obviously I set the other airmen up to complete the radio relay because we were having awful bad static on the radios. I could barely talk to the first patrolman that I had set by the logging road. I could barely hear him. I could not hear our control center at all.

The radio communications were being jammed by some unknown source according to the prior statement. The two most common causes of interference are transmitters and electrical equipment. Some common causes for interference would be:

- An intense radio signal from a nearby transmitter

- Unwanted signals (called spurious radiation) generated by the transmitting equipment

- Not enough shielding or filtering in the electronic equipment to prevent it from picking up unwanted signals

This would sound right since they were next to a craft of unknown nature, the craft being ten feet on three sides and eight feet tall, with unknown radio transmissions coming from inside the ship and unknown power supply. All of these would have caused the radios to malfunction.

As they got closer to the craft, it was triangular in shape. The top portion had mainly white light which encompassed most of the upper section of the craft. There was a small amount of white light appearing from the bottom of the craft. At the left side was a bluish light. And on the other side was red. The lights seem to be molded as part of the exterior of the structure.

As part of their job, they took pictures, mainly black and white, thirty-six pictures to a roll; when they were done with their investigation and returned to base, they would have turned the exposed rolls over to the base photo lab or base security. Because they were with the security unit, I would say they went to the base lab for developing.

Note: The base lab was operated under US Air Force guidelines; any images that were of any object of unknown nature would have been sealed and sent to Government Officials in the United States for examination. When the investigators would go and pick up the developed film they would have been told that nothing was exposed on the film.

Keep in mind that this is US soil in the UK – they would have only told the British officials probably ten percent of what happened. The other ninety percent would go through US channels, and that should be through USAF channels to 3ʳᵈ Air Force to MAJCOM (Major Air Command), which would have been at Ramstein AFB. Then Ramstein has procedures for reporting to JCS (Joint Chief of Staff) in the United States.

Sgt. James Penniston states:

> I did a full investigation of the downed craft. I mean I did a 360 degree walk around it. It was on the ground approximately 45 minutes, as part of the investigation I was able to touch the craft. The size of it was approximately 10 feet (3 meters) wide by 10 feet (3 meters) tall. The fabric or the shell was – I guess the best description would be a very smooth opaque, like black glass. Even though at a distance, it appeared metallic. It made no sense, once I was up there (close to it) that it was more like black glass. I'm not sure – I was pretty confused at that point.

Like most witnesses to a UFO sighting witnesses do not have the answers; all they have are questions and more questions.

Most people think that because a sighting is government related, there would be reason to wonder how much of a cover-up there is. When you start classifying information and you start saying, *We're not going to speak about this. We're following orders*, cover-ups can happen. When you're involved with it, unknowingly, you become a part of it.

Author's opinion: The opinions of the event differ from various witnesses. Some of the witnesses made a career of the military and stayed silent; their testimony seems to change from the time of the sighting event to now. Some witnesses left the service and their stories remained the same over the years. (Ref: Larry Warren, co-author of *Left at East Gate* – by the way, I personally believe this is a great book; thank you Peter Robbins.) When I initially heard about the Rendlesham case, I had never heard of a small triangular UFO before or the little crafts that came from within the larger craft. So I searched around the Internet forums looking for anything similar. And indeed, found UFO sightings, of people encountering small triangular UFOs, dating back to 1992-1993, and two of the sighting reports were made by amateur astronomers. One case was over a village in Cyprus, at very close range of a few meters, hovering outside his front door, at about his house's terrace level – he ran upstairs and saw the UFO from above as well. He described it as a "3m per side triangular craft with a low-pyramid on top; initially the sides of the craft looked like hundreds of very-very small yellow lights, which turned to red before it started to gain altitude and then shot upwards at bullet-like speed." The description of the craft seen in Cyprus matches quite accurately the Jim Penniston (USAF) drawing of the Rendlesham UFO in his report written in December 1980.

I will leave it up to the readers to decide the outcome of this sighting. Did the military cover it up? Did the military order these men to remain silent? Did the military change official documents in the cases where the military members refused to remain silent?

11

Nick Pope

and the MoD[42]

Nick Pope writes and commentates extensively in the media on conspiracy theories. This has included writing promotional material for 20th Century Fox, as part of the PR campaign for *The X-Files: I Want to Believe*.

Nick Pope worked for the British government for twenty-one years, at the Ministry of Defence. From 1991 to 1994 he ran the UK Ministry of Defence UFO project and common accusation is that the MoD was involved in a conspiracy and was covering up the truth about UFOs.

As with most Americans, Mr. Pope thinks the best-known conspiracy theories are probably those revolving around UFOs and Roswell. Mr. Pope was asked if he believed the conspiracy theories; he stated:

> I believe that many conspiracy theories arise because of fundamental misunderstandings of the way in which governments, the military, and intelligence agencies act. Others arise because facts and comments have been misunderstood or, in some cases, deliberately misrepresented.

The MoD's UFO project has its roots dating back to 1950. The Chief Scientific Adviser, Sir Henry Tizar, noted that UFO sightings shouldn't be dismissed out of hand without some form of proper scientific study. The Ministry of Defence has been investigating the UFO phenomenon and has received approximately 10,000 sighting reports to date. The objective hasn't really changed much. Their policy is to:

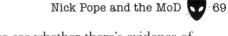

1. Investigate UFO sightings to see whether there's evidence of any threat to the defence of the UK.

2. Record the information that may be of any use, scientifically or militarily.

3. Having a UFO project in no way implies a corporate belief in extraterrestrial visitation.

4. To keep a watchful eye on our airspace.

5. Report anything operating in the United Kingdom's Air Defence Region.

The UK receives 200-300 reports each year, about the same as what New York receives. The methodology of an investigation is fairly standard worldwide:

1. Firstly, you interview the witness to obtain as much information as possible about the sighting:

   A. Date,

   B. Time,

   C. Location of the sighting,

   D. Description of the object,

   E. Its speed,

   F. Its height, etc.

2. Then you attempt to correlate the sighting with known aerial activity, such as civil flights, military exercises, or weather balloon launches.

3. You could check with the local observatory to see if astronomical phenomena such as meteors or fireballs might explain what was seen.

4. Check to see whether any UFOs that were seen were visually tracked on radar.

5. Study any photographs or video, you could.

In the UK, around eighty percent of UFO sightings could be explained as misidentifications of something ordinary, such as aircraft lights, satellites, airships, weather balloons, or planets. In around fifteen percent of cases, there was insufficient information to draw any firm conclusions. Approximately five percent of sightings seemed to defy conventional explanation. These percentages are the averages of all the sightings worldwide, most investigators will say five percent remain unsolved.

Mr. Pope was asked "What do you think about this five percent? Could they be extraterrestrial spacecraft? His reply was:

> I certainly can't rule out the possibility. There's some intriguing evidence, but no hard proof.

Unfortunately, Mr. Pope has never seen a UFO himself. My thinking is that busy people are constantly looking at their phones, iPads, newspaper, etc., and it seems they do not have the time to look up to gaze at the wonders of the universe.

There are aircraft and UAVs (both experimental and operational) – their existence in most countries is not yet public knowledge. But there are ways of eliminating this possibility from any official UFO investigations. To give one obvious example, if we know where they test fly their experimental craft, you can take this into account in any UFO investigation.

I have a lot of respect for Nick Pope. When he took office for the MoD, he signed a secrecy document that binds him for life, yet when you read his work or listen to him on the radio, it is obvious there is more than what he is saying, BUT since he cannot say it, it is up to us to use the clues we are given, and this is true with all government officials. Listen to what they say, then read between the lines.

12

Project Twinkle

Green fireballs are a type of unidentified flying object which have been sighted in the sky since the late 1940s. Early sightings primarily occurred in the southwestern United States, particularly in Arizona and New Mexico.

They were once of notable concern to the US government because they were often clustered around sensitive research and military installations, such as Los Alamos and Sandia National Laboratory, then Sandia Base – just as a large percent of UFO sightings are seen around our Military Nuclear facilities.

The strange green balls of light appeared suddenly and were reported many times per month near such New Mexico installations, but hardly anywhere else.

What caused these phenomena? Meteor expert conclusion was that the objects displayed too many anomalous characteristics to be a type of meteor and instead were artificial, perhaps secret Russian spy devices. The green fireballs were seen by many at Kirtland AFB, intelligence officers, and Air Command Defense personnel.

In December 1949, Project Twinkle, a network of green fireball observation and photographic stations, was established but never fully implemented. It was discontinued two years later, with the official conclusion that the phenomenon was probably natural in origin.

Green fireballs have been given natural, man-made, and extraterrestrial origins and have become associated with both the Cold War and ufology. Because of the extensive government paper trail on the phenomenon, many ufologists consider the green fireballs to be among the best documented examples of unidentified flying objects (UFOs).

A military crew described the light as like a huge green meteor except it arced upwards and then flat instead of downwards.

A civilian crew described the light as having a trajectory too low and flat for a meteor, at first abreast and ahead of them but then appearing to come straight at them on a collision course, forcing the pilot to swerve the plane at which time the object appeared full-moon size.

In addition, a dozen green fireballs were seen traveling generally north to south between 7:30 p.m. and 11:30 p.m. by security guards at military installations in the vicinity of Albuquerque and Las Vegas, New Mexico. The sightings near Albuquerque were at Sandia Base, a highly sensitive installation where atomic bombs were assembled near Kirtland Air Force Base. The next night, a similar green light was again spotted for a few seconds over Sandia Base.

The US Air Force Office of Special Investigations (AFOSI) at Kirtland AFB began an official inquiry, fearing the fireballs might be related to espionage and sabotage.

Two AFOSI investigators, both of whom were experienced pilots themselves, witnessed a green fireball while flying an aircraft the evening of December 8. They said:

- It was about 2,000 feet (610 m) above their craft.

- Roughly resembling the green flares commonly used by the Air Force, though "much more intense" and apparently "considerably brighter."

- The light seemed to burst into full brilliance almost instantaneously.

Their report stated a few notable points:

1. That the light was "definitely larger and more brilliant than a shooting star, meteor, or flare."

2. The light lasted only a few seconds, moving "almost flat and parallel to the earth."

3. The light's "trajectory then dropped off rapidly" leaving "a trail of fragments, reddish orange in color" which then fell towards the ground.

The next day, AFOSI consulted an astronomer from the University of New Mexico and a world renowned meteor expert who had previously worked on top-secret military projects. One of the consultants himself saw a "green fireball" on December 12, which was also seen at Los Alamos Scientific Laboratory, this enabled them to determine the trajectory using triangulation. From this, they discovered that the center of the trajectory was straight over Los Alamos.

In a classified letter to the Air Force on December 20, the consultants wrote that the object moved far too slowly to have been a meteor and left no "trail of sparks or dust cloud" as would be typical of meteors flying at low altitudes. Other anomalous characteristics were:

- The intense lime-green color

- Low altitude of only 8–10 miles

- Exhibiting no sound

- Flat rather than arced trajectory

- Turning on and off like a light switch

Later, they determined that the sightings were confined almost entirely to northern New Mexico, and no fragments were ever found despite extensive searches using triangulation techniques that had previously been successful in locating meteor fragments.

Other green fireball sightings occurred over Los Alamos on December 11, 13, 14, 20, 28, 1949 and January 6, 1950, raising the level of concern of security and military intelligence. The green fireball on December 20 was most remarkable in that it was seen to change direction, quite impossible for a meteor.

Two security officers saw it first descending at a forty-five-degree angle, then leveling off at an altitude of about two miles..

On January 13, 1950, the following message was sent to the Director of Army Intelligence from Fourth Army Headquarters in Texas:

> Agencies in New Mexico are greatly concerned . . .Some foreign power [may be] making "sensing shots" with some super-stratosphere device designed to be self-disintegrating . . . The phenomena [may be] the result of radiological warfare experiments by a foreign power . . . the rays may be lethal or might be . . . the cause of the plane crashes that have occurred recently . . . These incidents are of such great importance, especially as they are occurring in the vicinity of sensitive installations, that a scientific board [should] be sent...to study the situation.

On January 30, the brightest and most widely seen green fireball sighting occurred near Roswell, New Mexico. The next day, the FBI was informed by Army and Air Force intelligence that flying saucers and the fireballs were classified top secret.

Informal scientific study for the Air Force quickly became formal, being called the "Conference on Aerial Phenomena," convening at Los Alamos Scientific Laboratory in mid-February to review the data. The assembled people – both military personnel and civilian scientists – were informed that the fireballs were not the result of any secret military project.

They were absolutely convinced the green fireballs were not conventional fireballs or meteorites. They felt they could not be material objects because they made no sound and suggested they might be some unknown atmospheric electrical phenomena. In any event, though, they could not be foreign probes of some kind.

The scientists felt that a network of instrument stations should be established to photograph and analyze the fireballs. Despite the recommendation and the continuation of the green fireballs at a rate of about half a dozen a month, AFOSI oddly encountered both resistance and apathy from Air Force authorities responsible for setting up such a network.

By April 1949, similar sights were reported over a nuclear-weapons storage facility at Fort Hood in Texas. The intrusions were deemed so serious that, unlike the Air Force, the Army quickly set up an observation network.

The sightings continued until August, the most spectacular being on June 6 when a hovering orange light, 30 to 70 feet (21 m) across and a mile in the air, was spotted. Finally, it started moving in level flight and then burst into small particles.

On July 24, a green fireball was observed falling close to Socorro, New Mexico. Dust samples were collected at the School of Mines there and were found to contain large particles of copper. Scientists found this highly significant, since copper burns with the same yellow-green color characteristic of the green fireballs.

Note: If the copper particles came from the green fireballs, then they could not be conventional meteorites, since copper was never found in dust of meteoric origin.

Another Los Alamos conference convened on October 14. No one disputed the reality of the phenomena and nobody could explain it. Among the puzzles were the sudden onset and the high concentration of sightings in New Mexico, quite unlike natural phenomena. Despite this, it was decided the fireballs were probably atmospheric in origin. Instrumented observations – photographic, triangulation, and spectroscopic – were deemed essential to solving the mystery.

On November 3, Dr. Kaplan by this time had decided the fireballs might be a new type of rare meteor. Nonetheless, most of the scientists remained puzzled by the brightness, trajectories, and absence of sound. Seeming to contradict his meteor hypothesis, Kaplan also said:

This high selectivity of direction seems to indicate that some group was trying to pinpoint Los Alamos with a new sort of weapon.

This does not make any sense to an investigator. First, they stated it could not be a meteor, and then Dr. Kaplan said it's a rare meteor, and in the same breath stated that some group was trying to pinpoint Los Alamos with a new sort of weapon – which is it, meteor or weapon? Finally, on December 20, after nearly a year of foot-dragging, the instrument observation program was approved and Project Twinkle was born. The first instrument post (consisting of two officers) was established at Holloman Air Force Base in February 1950. Only one other instrument post was ever set up.

Over the objections of the consultants and others, the final report on Project Twinkle concluded the green lights were probably a natural event, maybe sunspot activity or an unusual concentration of meteors. The report stated:

> There has been no indication that even the somewhat strange observations often called "Green Fireballs" are anything but natural phenomena.

Twinkle was discontinued in December 1951.

Despite efforts of the final Twinkle report to downplay the fireballs and other studied UFO phenomena as natural, a follow-up report in February 1952 from the USAF Directorate of Intelligence disagreed:

> The Scientific Advisory Board Secretariat has suggested that this project not be declassified for a variety of reasons, chief among which is that no scientific explanation for any of the fireballs and other phenomena was revealed by the report and that some reputable scientists still believe that the observed phenomena are man-made.

It was also stated that some of the scientists continued to believe they were Russian spy devices. The following month, another letter from the Directorate of Intelligence to the Research Division of the Directorate of Research and Development again stated that the report should not be publicly released, since no real solution had been provided.

Despite the discontinuation of Project Twinkle, green fireballs were still occasionally sighted and LaPaz continued to comment. In early November, 1951, a month before the official termination of Twinkle, a huge flurry of green fireball sightings occurred in the Southwest and other states. A recent green fireball incident over Arizona from November 1951 was mentioned. Another sighting near Roswell, New Mexico, on July 10, 1947, which was about the same time as the famous Roswell UFO incident.

Birds aren't the only things dropping from the sky these days: A huge emerald fireball in the sky spooked people who saw it in the Southern US, with sightings reported from Oklahoma to the Florida panhandle. It turns out that it was a meteor strike, which hit somewhere near Poteau Mountain in Oklahoma. It burned green briefly, which likely means it contained copper.

13

If UFOs are No Threat to Our Nation's Security, Why Would the Military be Creating Weapons Against Aliens?

The United States military are preparing weapons which could be used against the aliens. Could this get us into an intergalactic war without us ever having any warning?

We should be concerned about the consequences of starting an intergalactic war. Now is the time for open disclosure – are there Extraterrestrial civilizations visiting Earth.

There are a few questions/issues that we should be asking our governments officials worldwide:

1. Why do governments feel the need for disclosure and secrecy?

2. If we get into an Intergalactic war, what are our odds of winning?

3. Shouldn't our governments need to openly address the important issues surrounding the possible deployment of weapons in outer space?

4. Should the people of Earth know of any war plans against ethical Extraterrestrial societies?

5. Are there any advanced extraterrestrial civilizations that may now be visiting Earth?

Should we be concerned about what the consequences might be of starting an intergalactic war?

The secrecy involved in all matters pertaining to the Roswell incident is nothing compared to what we could be facing. The classification was, from the outset, above top secret, so the vast majority of US officials and politicians, let alone civilians, were never in-the-loop.

The Bush administration finally agreed to let the military build a forward base on the moon. This will put us in a better position to keep track of the movements of visitors from space, and to shoot at them, if military so decides.

> The time has come to lift the veil of secrecy, and let the truth emerge; the people of the earth have a right to know. We need a real and informative debate, about one of the most important problems facing our planet today.

The Disclosure Project, a US-based organization that has assembled high-level military intelligence witnesses of a possible ET presence, is one of the organizations we should receive answers from.

The United Nations agreed, in 1967, that weapons of mass destruction must not be based in space. Has the time come to extend this ban to all weapons? And why would we even consider placing weapons of mass destruction in space if the governments do not believe aliens exists?

The time has come to inform the politicians in Washington that they need to do their job; they work for the American people, not the parties they represent. They seem to forget that once elected into office they are not democrats, republicans, tea party, or whatever; they represent the PARTY OF THE PEOPLE.

The above statement is not only for people of the United States, it is for every human being who lives on this great planet. It is time the governments around the world learn that they represent human lives, everywhere.

For every action there is a reaction. Governments need to consider the consequences before jumping in blind on costly projects. Information is always best; inform your citizens – they may be more help than you can imagine.

14

The Kinross Incident

First Lieutenant Felix Eugene Moncla, Jr. was a United States Air Force pilot who mysteriously disappeared while pursuing an unidentified flying object over Lake Superior in 1953. First Lieutenant Moncla was on temporary assignment at Kinross Air Force Base, when he disappeared.

The US Air Force reported that Moncla had crashed and that the "unknown" object was a misidentified Royal Canadian Air Force aircraft. On multiple occasions, the RCAF refuted their involvement in the intercept, in correspondence with members of the public asking for further details on the intercept.[56]

Air Defense Command Ground Intercept radar operators at Sault Ste. Marie, Michigan, identified an unusual target near the Sault Locks, located on the St. Mary River. An F-89C Scorpion jet from Kincheloe Air Force Base known as Kinross Air Force Base, was scrambled to investigate the radar return; the Scorpion was piloted by First Lieutenant Moncla with Second Lieutenant Robert L. Wilson acting as the Scorpion's radar operator.

Second Lieutenant Wilson had problems tracking the object on the Scorpion's radar, so ground radar operators at Air Defense Command gave Moncla directions towards the object as he flew. Flying at a speed of 500 miles per hour, Moncla eventually closed in on the object at about 8,000 feet in altitude.

Ground Control tracked the Scorpion and the unidentified object as two "blips" on the radar screen. The two blips on the radar screen grew closer and closer, until they seemed to merge as one.

Ground control assumed that Moncla had flown either under or over the target. Ground Control thought that moments later, the Scorpion and the object would again appear as two separate blips. The thought soon became a fear that the two objects had struck one another "as if in a smashing collision."[57]

Suddenly, the single blip disappeared from the radar screen, and there was no return at all. Attempts were made to contact Moncla via radio, but was unsuccessful. A search and rescue operation was quickly mounted, but found not a trace of the plane or the pilots.

USAF Accident Investigation Report

(See Appendix D)

The official USAF Accident Investigation Report states the F-89 was sent to investigate an RCAF C-47 Skytrain which was traveling off course. (Sounds different than the orders First Lieutenant Felix Eugene Moncla, Jr. received when he was sent up to investigate...)

The IFF signal (identifying friend or foe) also disappeared after the two returns merged on the radar scope. Although efforts to contact the crew on radio were unsuccessful, the pilot of another F-89 sent on the search stated in testimony to the Accident Board that he believed that he had heard a brief radio transmission from the pilot about forty minutes after the plane disappeared.[58]

Air Force investigators reported that Moncla may have experienced vertigo and crashed into the lake. The Air Force said that Moncla had been known to experience vertigo from time to time.

Author's Note: Vertigo is a type of dizziness, where there is a feeling of motion when one is stationary. The symptoms are usually due to a dysfunction of the vestibular system in the inner ear. Pilots are grounded when they are known to have this.

It was later discovered that statements had been made by former members of Lt. Moncla's organization; these were not first-hand evidence and were regarded as hearsay.

Contradictions in Official USAF Explanations

The official accident report states that when the unknown object was first picked up on radar, it was believed to be RCAF aircraft "VC-912," but it was classified as "UNKNOWN" because it was off its flight plan course by about thirty miles.[60] The pilot of this RCAF flight, Gerald Fosberg, denies these allegations.

The USAF also provided an alternative explanation that the unknown in that case was a Canadian DC-3. "It was over the locks by mistake." The "locks" refers to the restricted air space over the locks at Sault Ste. Marie, on the US Canadian border at the southeast end of Lake Superior.

Update: November 1, 2006

A number of individuals have been trying to corroborate information supplied by Adam Jimenez, who is the contact for Great Lakes Dive Company (if such a group actually exists). Most of the investigators believe that the information which has surfaced in these investigations suggests that this find is possibly or probably a hoax. Adam Jimenez is currently unavailable for comment or to answer questions. He is the only person known who can substantiate his claims.

The Great Lakes Dive Company has announced that they have found the wreck of an F-89 on the bottom of Lake Superior. Using advanced side scan sonar equipment, they surveyed an area around the location where the F-89 was last observed on radar, back on the night it disappeared, November 23, 1953.

Note: If an F-89 flying at a speed of 500 miles per hour hit another craft, there would be two piles of debris. There would not be an almost complete F-89, resting upright on the lakebed with the nose and one wingtip buried in the sediment.

Great Lakes Dive Company were contacted by the Canadian government who asked them to provide the GPS coordinates of the site before they would allow them to finish their site surveys. They requested that a Coast Guard vessel or Canadian government official accompany Great Lakes Dive Company on any further surveys of the site.

Great Lakes Dive Company believes this discovery may imply the F-89 was brought down by a collision with some sort of unknown craft which may be the mysterious object on the lakebed. However they are unable to reconcile this theory with good structural condition of the F-89.

Is it possible that the missing tail piece was part of the parts found in 1968? We may never be able to find out as the identification of the parts were apparently withheld from the public and the Canadian and US governments claim they have no records of the find.

I believe the family of the missing USAF crew clearly have a right to know whether the discovered wreck contains the remains of their missing family.

See Appendix D for the following:

1. Picture of Lt. Gene Moncla by T-33 at Truax Field in Madison, WI
2. Two blips appear to merge, then both vanish
3. Newspaper reports of crash
4. USAF Accident Investigation Report

Form 14 - Informal Report

- Lt. Stuart's statement
- Capt. Bridge's statement
- Statement made by Lt. Mingenbach
- Statement made by Lt. Nordeck
- Maintenance reports and forms

15

Astronaut Buzz Aldrin

Buzz Aldrin is a mechanical engineer, retired United States Air Force pilot, and astronaut who was the pilot of the Lunar Module on Apollo 11, the first manned lunar landing in history. On July 20, 1969, he was the second human being to set foot on the moon; Neil Armstrong was the first person to step on the moon.

In 2005, Aldrin told an interviewer that they saw an unidentified flying object. The statements that were made after Aldrin came public are that he probably was seeing one of four detached spacecraft adapter panels, but the upper stage was 6,000 miles away, and the four panels were jettisoned before the S-IVB made its separation maneuver so they would closely follow the Apollo 11 spacecraft until its first mid-course correction.

Aldrin confirmed that there was no such sighting of anything deemed extraterrestrial, and said they were, and are, "99.9 percent" sure that the object was the detached panel.

Why would Buzz Aldrin change his statement from his original sighting report? Could it be the government put pressure on him? He was retired so he was pulling a pension from the government – did they threaten to stop his pension?

According to Aldrin, he mentioned seeing unidentified objects, and he claims his words were taken out of context; he asked the Science Channel to clarify to viewers he did not see alien spacecraft, but they refused.

Aldrin had an exciting military career:

1. He graduated third in his class at West Point in 1951 with a B.S. in mechanical engineering.

2. Was commissioned as a Second Lieutenant in the US Air Force.

Buzz Aldrin

3. Served as a jet fighter pilot during the Korean War.

4. He flew 66 combat missions in F-86 Sabres.

5. Aldrin shot down two Mikoyan-Gurevich MiG-15 aircraft.

6. After the war, Aldrin was assigned as an aerial gunnery instructor at Nellis Air Force Base in Nevada.

7. He was an aide to the dean of faculty at the US Air Force Academy.

8. He flew F-100 Super Sabres as a flight commander at Bitburg Air Base, Germany in the 22nd Fighter Squadron.

9. He then earned his Sc.D. degree in Astronautics from MIT.

10. On completion of his doctorate, he was assigned to the Gemini Target Office of the Air Force Space Systems Division in Los Angeles.

11. He was selected as an astronaut.

NASA Career

Aldrin was selected as part of the third group of NASA astronauts in October 1963. Test pilot experience was no longer a requirement, so this was the first selection that he was eligible for.

After the untimely deaths of the original Gemini 9 prime crew, Aldrin was promoted with Jim Lovell as back-up crew for the mission. The main objective of the revised mission (Gemini 9A) was to rendezvous and dock with a target vehicle, but this failed.

Aldrin suggested an effective exercise for the craft to come together into one place with a coordinate in space. He was confirmed as pilot on Gemini 12, the last Gemini mission and the last chance to prove methods for EVA. Aldrin set a record for extra-vehicular activity and proved that astronauts could work outside spacecraft.

On July 20, 1969, Aldrin was the second astronaut to walk on the moon and the first to have also spacewalked, keeping his record total EVA time until that was surpassed on Apollo 14. There was also a desire on NASA's part for the first person to step onto the Moon's surface to be a civilian, which Armstrong was.

Buzz Aldrin was the first person to hold a religious ceremony on the Moon. After landing on the moon, Aldrin radioed Earth:

I'd like to take this opportunity to ask every person listening in, whoever and wherever they may be, to pause for a moment and contemplate the events of the past few hours, and to give thanks in his or her own way.

He gave himself Communion on the surface of the Moon, but he kept it secret because of a possibility of a lawsuit. Aldrin, a Freemason, also carried to the Moon a special deputation from Grand Master J. Guy Smith, with which to claim Masonic territorial jurisdiction over the Moon on behalf of the Grand Lodge of Texas.

Unfortunately many questions still remain:

1. Did Buzz Aldrin change his view in seeing a UFO due to military influence?

2. Was the object really the detached panel?

3. Why would the Masons want territorial jurisdiction on the moon?

4. Did man really land on the moon?

5. Were we alone on the moon?

16

Ed White and James McDivitt
The Gemini 4 UFO

Of the millions of UFO witnesses worldwide, probably the most reputable and respected are American astronauts. And of the dozens of reports associating astronauts with UFO encounters and photographs, undoubtedly the best was the June 4, 1965 sighting reported by Maj. James McDivitt, command pilot of the two-man Gemini-4. His testimony baffled even the super-skeptical Condon Committee in 1969; a photograph from his flight has been widely hailed as one of the "best UFO photos ever made."

McDivitt never made much of his sighting, however often he has retold the tale to audiences and interviewers. There is no evidence anybody took the slightest official notice, nor is there any record that the astronaut ever filed a UFO report with Project Blue Book.

NASA has always insisted that there was nothing at all mysterious about the encounter and that the object was clearly terrestrial in origin. McDivitt's own booster rocket has been tagged as the culprit in some studies.

The facts are plain. On June 3, 1965, Gemini-4 was launched into orbit 150 miles above the Earth's surface. Rookie astronauts McDivitt and White were headed for the USA's first long-duration flight, the first to attempt for extensive visual observations and photography. On the second day, over Hawaii, the 35-year-old McDivitt reported seeing an object – "like a beer can with an arm sticking out." Together with a mysterious "tadpole" photo, the McDivitt report has achieved UFO superstardom and has been firmly enshrined in UFO literature and folklore.

McDivitt himself described it as:

> I was flying with Ed White. He was sleeping at the time so I don't have anybody to verify my story. We were drifting in space with the control engines shut down and all the instrumentation off when suddenly an object appeared in the window. It had a very definite shape – a cylindrical object – it was white – it had a long arm that stuck out on the side. I don't know whether it was a very small object up close or a very large object a long ways away. There was nothing to judge by. I really don't know how big it was. We had two cameras that were just floating in the spacecraft at the time, so I grabbed one and took a picture of the object and grabbed the other and took a picture. Then I turned on the rocket control systems because I was afraid we might hit it. At the time we were drifting – without checking I have no idea which way we were going – but as we drifted up a little farther the sun shone on the window of the spacecraft. The windshield was dirty – just like in an automobile, you can't see through it. So I had the rocket control engines going again and moved the spacecraft so that the window was in darkness again – the object was gone. I called down later and told them what had happened and they went back and checked their records of other space debris that was flying around but we were never able to identify what it could have been. The film was sent back to NASA and reviewed by some NASA film technicians. One of them selected what he thought was what we talked about, at least before I had a chance to review it. It was not the picture – it was a picture of a sun reflection on the window.

In 1968, the Air Force seemed anxious to wash its hands of the UFO business and find justification for closing down "Project Blue Book." The University of Colorado was contracted to make a study of the whole UFO phenomenon under the direction of Professor Condon. Most ufologers regard the "Condon Report" as a whitewash of the Air Force's role and as a deliberate attempt to slant evidence to fit a preconceived conclusion. Yet the Condon Commitee endorsed the McDivitt UFO sighting.

But since 1969, when the Condon Report was published, some new resources have become available concerning McDivitt's UFO.

The booster did not decay for at least fifty hours, according to tracking data later released by NORAD via the Goddard Space Flight Center. During that time it was close to the Gemini and then gradually pulled ahead of it on its decaying orbit. It was well within the 1,000 mile range specified by NORAD, yet it was not on the list of nearby satellites. Why not?

A reasonable hypothesis is that NASA had only asked about all other space objects, not specifying any debris associated with the Gemini itself. The NORAD computers would produce reports for only satellites launched before Gemini-4, ignoring any objects launched with it. Alternately, NORAD might not even have had accurate data on the booster, since most of its radars were in northern regions optimal for spotting Soviet space vehicles but beyond the range of American manned spacecraft. In 1965, NORAD had only one radar site which could have tracked satellites in the Gemini orbit.

There were reports that the UFO was really a secret US military reconnaissance satellite and that space officials had been unable to identify it because the Department of Defense refused to admit the existence of such a satellite.

At a news conference on June 11th, McDivitt gave more details about the object:

> Near Hawaii...I saw a white object and it looked like it was cylindrical and it looked to me like there was a white arm sticking out of it.... It looked a lot like an upper stage of a booster.

Years later, McDivitt became something of a celebrity to UFO groups with his short modest story of a space UFO, McDivitt related that:

> I just happened to look out the window and there in front of me was an object which was cylindrical in shape and had a pole sticking out there. It would be about the same relative shape as a beer can with a pencil sticking out one corner of it.

The Air Force wasn't interested, either: McDivitt never even filed a UFO report with Project Blue Book or anyone else. NASA did not bother with the story, it seems, because nobody was particularly puzzled by the object. NASA Assistant Administrator for Legislative Affairs, Richard L. Callaghan, replied that, "We believe it to be a rocket tank or spent second stage of a rocket."

Keeping in mind that astronaut White, who had spent the same period watching the same booster, had already misidentified it at least once at a much closer range. Let us take another look at the visual conditions under which McDivitt saw the object and consider if he might have made a mistake.

The smeared windows (White tried to clean them when he was outside the capsule but only made them worse) can certainly be a hindrance for visual identification of objects.

The "McDivitt UFO photo" – the "tadpole" – had a life entirely apart from the actual McDivitt UFO report. When pressed by newsmen for the photo which McDivitt had reportedly taken of the object, officials at the Public Affairs Office at NASA headquarters went through the flight film and selected a series of shots which they thought might have been the object. This was before McDivitt had a chance to review the film himself.

The original NASA caption on the photo (PAO 65-H-1013) was as follows:

> This photograph...shows the satellite McDivitt observed on the 20th revolution of his four-day space flight.... He said the Gemini-4 spacecraft was turning and the sun was coming across the window when he filmed the object.

Later, after consultation with the astronaut, NASA press officials changed the caption to read:

> Astronaut James McDivitt photographed this sun flare through the spacecraft window.... McDivitt explained later after the flight that the sun was coming across the window as the spacecraft rolled, the sun rays struck a metal bolt, causing the flares in the camera lens.

Once the Condon committee had endorsed McDivitt's UFO in 1969, the reputation of the photograph grew. Often reprinted in UFO books and magazines, it became an important piece of UFO evidence. In 1975, NICAP in Washington, D.C. selected it as one of the four best UFO photographs ever made. Their choice was based on a penciled note on the back of their print, which reported that McDivitt had told someone that this showed his UFO. Nobody at NICAP could remember when or where.

17

Astronaut Robert White

Bob White is convinced his story deserves a grand stage, that his most prized possession should be displayed before a national audience. It should draw tourists from all over the country, he figures, and be a major attraction for people who want to see an artifact that White swears was retrieved from a UFO in 1985.[119]

Instead, White's find is in tiny Reeds Spring in southwestern Missouri, secured in a locked display case at Museum of the Unexplained, a converted video-rental store that, during a recent morning, went more than three hours without a customer. White can't figure it out. All he wants to do is find some believers. He wants people to quit snickering and looking at him as if he's crazy. He wants them to listen to his story, to take a hard look at his metallic artifact, to give him a chance.

White said, "This is the most difficult thing I've ever done in my life." The odds are stacked against him. He and his partner at the museum, Robert Gibbons, have been rejected and ridiculed. White estimates he has spent more than $60,000 traveling to conferences, starting the museum, having the artifact tested and retested. And yet he forges on.

"I'm 73 years old," White said. "I don't have much longer. What I'd like to see before I'm gone is the national media get their heads out of their..." White paused, choosing his words carefully, "...out of the sand. I'd like to see the national media and everybody else realize that what I have is real." Scientists theorize that the "UFO" lights that White said he encountered could have been nothing more than a meteorite, that his artifact could be space debris. Some scientists who have tested the object said there was nothing extraterrestrial about it.[120]

Ask White whether he believed in unidentified flying objects prior to 1985, and he scrunches up his nose. "Never," he said. "Not a bit. I was the biggest skeptic in the world." That all changed overnight. Here's how it is remembered:

> White and a friend were driving from Denver to Las Vegas on a desolate highway near the Colorado-Utah border. It was 2 or 3 a.m., he said, and White was sleeping in the passenger seat. At one point, his friend woke him up and pointed out a strange light in the distance. White didn't think much of it and went back to sleep. Then his friend woke him up again. This time, White said the lights were blinding.
>
> He got out of the car and stared, dumbfounded. The object was about 100 yards in front of him, and it was huge...absolutely huge." In time, the lights bolted toward the sky and connected with a pair of neon, tubular lights – "the mother ship," White guesses now. And just like that, he said, the entire contraption zipped eastward through the Colorado sky and disappeared.
>
> "What I saw, was not of this Earth." As the craft flew away, White said, he noticed an orange light falling to the ground. Could it be a locator probe? Something broke off. It was red hot when he reached it, he said, but in time it cooled enough to pick up. White shoved the object into the trunk of the car.

The object is about 7-1/2 inches long and shaped like a teardrop. It has a coarse, metallic exterior and weighs less than 2 pounds. It looks a bit like it could be a petrified pine cone and is composed primarily of aluminum. White has had the item tested several times, hoping for some answers. The Nevada-based National Institute for Discovery Science in 1996 sent a sample of the object to the New Mexico Institute of Mining and Technology. "The metallurgical analysis was pretty mundane," said Colm Kelleher, a scientist at the National Institute for Discovery Science. "We didn't find any evidence that it was extraterrestrial. Now you can make the argument that we didn't spend $1 million and look at every conceivable option. We didn't cover every base."

Another scientist who tested it at a California laboratory – and who asked that his name and that of the laboratory not be used – said, "It didn't show any extraterrestrial signature."

Sgt. Gary Carpenter, who works at the North American Aerospace Defense Command in Colorado Springs, Colorado, said it was not uncommon for NORAD to get calls about strange lights and unidentified objects. Not once, he said, has the object been identified as an alien spacecraft. "Usually it turns out to be space debris from a satellite that's decaying, or it's in the realm of naturally occurring, celestial lights," he said. "It could be something like a falling star. It could be contrails, the things you would see trailing an aircraft."

White opened the Museum of the Unexplained with visions of turning it into a destination. He wasn't looking to get rich – according to the Missouri secretary of state's office, the museum was registered as a nonprofit organization in August 2000 – but he hoped to spread the word about his experience. Exhibits include a keyboard from the movie *Men in Black II* in which the shift key doesn't capitalize or de-capitalize but translates from English to an alien language. Other exhibits are little more than newspaper articles or passages from the Internet affixed to the wall with thumb tacks.

Said White,

> I don't know what I have to do to prove this is the truth. You can't make this stuff up.

Update:

Museum of the Unexplained Test Results Match Extraterrestrial Findings from Mars Artifacts.

Did Bob White's UFO Object Come From Mars? Origin May Have Been Found For Recovered UFO Material.

FOR IMMEDIATE RELEASE

Researchers and scientists at the Museum of the Unexplained are excited about startling new revelations about Bob White's mysterious "object" recovered from a UFO encounter in 1985 near Grand Junction, Colorado. Bob's object has been tested at the Los Alamos National Laboratory, New Mexico Tech, and at the Geosciences Research Division of the Scripps Institute in La Jolla, California.

Dr. Robert Gibbons, former scientist with NASA, and current Executive Director of the Museum, made this statement.

> We recently came across scientific data that linked Bob's object with the planet Mars. Isotope abundance ratio tests were performed on Bob's object in May 1999 in La Jolla, California and the numbers are virtually the same as obtained from Martian meteorite samples. The ratio of isotopes of Strontium for the QUE 94201 meteorite found in Antarctica in 1994 was 0.701. The ratio of isotopes of Strontium for Bob's object was 0.712. The ratio of isotopes of Strontium for the Shergotty meteorite found India in

1865 was 0.723. Bob's object is right in the middle of two proven Martian meteorites!

The Martian meteorite data came from a scientific paper published on the website of the Planetary Science Research Discoveries, an educational website supported by NASA's Office of Space Sciences and by the Hawaii Space Grant Consortium. Dr. Gibbons is calling for more scientific tests on the Bob White object to prove its origin once and for all.

18

Astronaut Donald Slayton

 Donald Slayton, a Mercury astronaut, revealed in an interview he had seen UFOs in 1951:

> I was testing a P-51 fighter in Minneapolis when I spotted this object. I was at about 10,000 feet on a nice, bright, sunny afternoon. I thought the object was a kite, then I realized that no kite is going to fly that high.
>
> As I got closer, it looked like a weather balloon, grey and about three feet in diameter. But as soon as I got behind the darn thing it didn't look like a balloon anymore. It looked like a saucer, a disk. About the same time, I realized that it was suddenly going away from me - and there I was, running at about 300 miles per hour. I tracked it for a little way, and then all of a sudden the damn thing just took off. It pulled about a 45-degree climbing turn and accelerated and the object flat disappeared.

Donald Kent "Deke" Slayton (March 1, 1924 – June 13, 1993) was one of the original NASA Mercury Seven astronauts. After initially being grounded by a heart murmur, he served as NASA's Director of Flight Crew Operations, making him responsible for crew assignments at NASA from November 1963 until March 1972. At that time, he was granted medical clearance to fly as the docking module pilot of the Apollo-Soyuz Test Project. At the age of 51, he became the oldest person to fly into space. This record was surpassed decades later by his NASA classmate John Glenn, at the age of 77, on STS-95.

NASA STS 95. *Courtesy of NASA, photo of Discovery in flight*

STS-95 (John Glenn's mission at age 77)

Mission: John Glenn's Flight; SPACEHAB

Space Shuttle: Discovery

Launch Pad: 39B

Launched: October 29, 1998, 2:19:34 p.m. EST

Landing Site: Kennedy Space Center, Florida

Landing: November 7, 1998, 12:04:00 p.m. EST

Runway: 33

Rollout Distance: 9,508 feet

Rollout Time: 59 seconds

Revolution: 134

Mission Duration: 9 days, 19 hours, 54 minutes, 2 seconds

Orbit Altitude: 310 nautical miles

Orbit Inclination: 28.45 degrees

Miles Traveled: 3.6 million

On December 12, 1951, Slayton had an extraordinary aerial experience while testing out a P-51 Mustang in the skies over Minnesota. He described it in his 1995 autobiography, *Deke!*:

> I realized I wasn't closing on that son of a bitch. A P-51 at that time would cruise at 280 miles an hour. But this thing just kept going and climbing at the same time at about a forty-five-degree climb. I kept trying to follow it, but he just left me behind and flat disappeared. The guys on the ground tracked it with a theodolite, and they'd computed the speed at 4,000 miles an hour.

This is a simply amazing UFO incident considering both Slayton's resume and the speed of the UFO. To put it in context, the SR-71 Blackbird, which wasn't introduced until more than a decade later and was the fastest plane in the world in its day and long after, topped out at around 2,200 mph. The hovering and then hitting that speed in apparently very short order is really astonishing. The forty-five degree climb Slayton describes is a clear signature of a high performance aircraft.

Slayton goes on to mention in his account that he often wondered if his report made it into Project Blue Book. Well it did! And that makes this case doubly compelling. I think it's important to consider that when you're recounting an event, who the audience is matters. If it's a casual conversation, the story might go one way; if it's for a formal report or part of a book or article or a media interview, it could go quite differently.

On page 663 of the Blue Book archive, investigator Major Gerhard Kaske wrote:

> The pilot assumes the speed of the object at this point was about 380 to 400 mph.

Discrepancies don't necessarily equal dishonesty but the difference between 400 mph and 4,000 mphH is not within any reasonable margin for error.

If Slayton assumed much higher then he would have been making a pretty bold statement considering the speed of planes in those days. Slayton was already a very experienced pilot at that point, having flown 56 combat missions during World War II, had a degree in aeronautical engineering from the University of Minnesota, and was well on his way to testing supersonic aircraft at Edwards Air Force base before ultimately joining NASA. He was well aware of what contemporary aircraft were capable of.

The math doesn't check out for the object to flat out disappear in the three to four minutes Slayton said the incident took place in at 380 to 400 mph, not with excellent visibility that day. The Blue Book investigators determined Slayton had seen a balloon, but winds in the upper atmosphere top out at about 250 mph, so even with a conservative speed estimate of around 400 mph along with the change in speed Slayton describes in both his biography and official account, that explanation just doesn't hold up.

Did he deliberately low ball the speed in the report? Slayton himself said he had to be talked into making a report. He made the report a week after the incident. Of course a stone-cold debunker might say he exaggerated his account in the book to make for a better read but considering the totality of his lifetime of accomplishments and the small portion his UFO sighting takes up in his biography, that's highly unlikely.

Slayton also mentions in his bio that the UFO crowd had latched onto a couple innocuous events during space flights, but there was really nothing there. I'm not sure which ones he's talking about specifically. I did see an interview with Martyn Stubbs where he actually talks about the John Glenn "fireflies" incident as if that was still a UFO, although it technically wasn't until Scott Carpenter figured out it was only frost flaking from the capsule on the next flight.

The Glenn incident is covered in some detail in the Academy Award winning 1983 film *The Right Stuff*, which features Slayton prominently as well. When it comes to astronauts and UFOs, it's the usual mixed bag you get with the UFO phenomenon, isn't it? A little bit of everything that only intensifies the mystery. You've got Edgar Mitchell, who makes no claim of a direct UFO encounter but is adamant about alien visitation. You've got Gordon Cooper who was adamant about his own encounters in particular and alien visitation in general. And you've got Deke Slayton who reported initially and wrote about a UFO encounter but declined to attempt to explain it himself. "I don't know what it was," he wrote in his biography. "It was unidentified."

The Deke Slayton case is one of the most underrated of all UFO cases. The witness had impeccable credentials as an aviator and continued on to a distinguished career as a space pioneer, a true American hero. His autobiographical account is consistent with his initial report in its essential elements and where it strays is both explainable and understandable.

19

Disclosure from Astronaut Gordon Cooper

I believe that these extraterrestrial vehicles and their crews are visiting this planet from other planets, which are a little more technically advanced than we are on Earth. I feel that we need to have a top level, coordinated program to scientifically collect and analyze data from all over the Earth concerning any type of encounter, and to determine how best to interfere with these visitors in a friendly fashion.

Astronaut Gordon Cooper
Message to the UN

 Why would an astronaut put his reputation on the line by creating such a message? This just shows that the government knows more than they are letting on, and some respected citizens are speaking up.

We may first have to show them that we have learned how to resolve our problems by peaceful means rather than warfare, before we are accepted as fully qualified universal team members. Their acceptance will have tremendous possibilities of advancing our world in all areas. Certainly then it would seem that the UN has a vested interest in handling the subject quickly and properly.

I should point out that I am not an experienced UFO professional researcher – I have not as yet had the privilege of flying a UFO nor of meeting the crew of one. However, I do feel that I am somewhat qualified to discuss them, since I have been into the fringes of the vast areas of which they travel. Also, I did have occasion in 1951 to have two days of observation of many flights of them, of different sizes flying in fighter formation, generally from west to east over Europe. They were at a higher altitude than we could reach with our jet fighters....

If the UN agrees to pursue this project and lend the credibility to it, perhaps many more well qualified people will agree to step forth and provide help and information.

~Astronaut Gordon Cooper

Addressing a UN panel discussion on UFOs and ETs in New York, in 1985; Panel was chaired by then UN Secretary-General Kurt Waldheim.

Leroy Gordon Cooper, was one of the nation's first astronauts who once set a space endurance record by traveling more than 3.3 million miles aboard Gemini 5 in 1965. He died on Monday October 4, 2004. He was 77.

"As one of the original seven Mercury astronauts, Gordon Cooper was one of the faces of America's fledgling space program. He truly portrayed the right stuff, and he helped gain the backing and enthusiasm of the American public, so critical for the spirit of exploration," NASA Administrator Sean O'Keefe said on the space agency's website.

Cooper, an Oklahoma native who entered the Marine Corps after graduating from high school in 1945, later became an elite Air Force test pilot at Edwards Air Force Base in California, where he became fascinated with the space program. In April 1959, Cooper was named as one of the Project Mercury astronauts, following grueling physical and mental tests each candidate had to endure. At the news conference naming the future of America's space program, Cooper was joined by Alan Shepard, Gus Grissom, John Glenn, M. Scott Carpenter, Walter Schirra, Jr. and Deke Slayton.

On May 15 and 16, 1963, Cooper piloted the Faith 7 spacecraft:

1. A 22-orbit mission that concluded the operational phase of Project Mercury.

2. Two years later, he would set a new space endurance record, serving as command pilot of the eight-day, 120-revolution Gemini 5 mission, which began August 21, 1965.

3. On this flight, he and Charles Conrad traveled a distance of 3,312,993 miles in 190 hours and 56 minutes.

4. Cooper also became the first man to make a second orbital flight.

5. During his two space flights, Cooper logged 225 hours, 15 minutes and 3 seconds.

6. He served as backup command pilot for Gemini 12; and

7. As backup commander for Apollo X.

8. Cooper logged more than 7,000 hours flying time in jets and commercial aircraft.

9. He retired from the Air Force and NASA in 1970 with the rank of colonel.

Concerning UFOs

In his post-NASA career, Cooper became known as an outspoken believer in UFOs and charged that the government was covering up its knowledge of extraterrestrial activity. "I believe that these extraterrestrial vehicles and their crews are visiting this planet from other planets, which obviously are a little more technically advanced than we are here on Earth," he told a United Nations panel in 1985.

> I feel that we need to have a top-level, coordinated program to scientifically collect and analyze data from all over the Earth concerning any type of encounter, and to determine how best to interface with these visitors in a friendly fashion.

He added,

> For many years I have lived with a secret, in a secrecy imposed on all specialists and astronauts. I can now reveal that every day, in the USA, our radar instruments capture objects of form and composition unknown to us.

"There certainly have been too many people, very qualified people and qualified groups of people, that have had interface of one type or another with extraterrestrial craft or beings," Cooper said. "To really deny that something is going on and deny that they definitely exist... we need a little more explanation."

Cooper tells how he saw his first UFO over Europe in 1951. An Air Force pilot in West Germany, Cooper and his squadron mates were scrambled in their F-86 Sabre jets to intercept what appeared to be several metallic silver and saucer-shaped craft.

Cooper also describes an incident at Edwards Air Force Base, California, in which he once looked at film of a crashed UFO in the

American Southwest taken in the late 1950s. That film, he writes, was whisked away to the Pentagon never to be seen or heard of again.

The former astronaut argues for the government to open up its files and come clean about alien visitations. So convinced is Cooper that UFOs deserve serious study that he once testified before the United Nations in 1978 on the topic. His hope was that the U.N. would become a central repository for accounts of UFO sightings. "I made the effort to get the U.N. to pick up the ball," Cooper said. "They thought it was a great idea, but they never did anything about it."

And there are thousands of witness reports and a quantity of documents to prove this, but nobody wants to make them public. Why? Because the authorities are afraid that people may think them some kind of horrible invaders.

Cooper states:

> As far as I am concerned, there have been too many unexplained examples of UFO sightings around this Earth for us to rule out the possibilities that some form of life exists out there beyond our own world.

In 1957, Cooper was one of an elite band of test pilots at Edwards Air Force Base in California, in charge of several advanced projects, including the installation of a precision landing system.

> I had a camera crew filming the installation when they spotted a saucer. They filmed it as it flew overhead, then hovered, extended three legs as landing gear, and slowly came down to land on a dry lake bed!
>
> These guys were all pro cameramen, so the picture quality was very good.
>
> The camera crew managed to get within 20 or 30 yards of it, filming all the time. It was a classic saucer, shiny silver and smooth, about 30 feet across. It was pretty clear it was an alien craft.
>
> As they approached closer it took off.

When his camera crew handed over the film, Cooper followed standard procedure and contacted Washington to report the UFO and "all heck broke loose."

After awhile a high-ranking officer said when the film was developed I was to put it in a pouch and send it to Washington.

> He didn't say anything about me not looking at the film. That's what I did when it came back from the lab and it was all there just like the camera crew reported.

When the Air Force later started Operation Blue Book to collate UFO evidence and reports, Cooper says he mentioned the film evidence.

> But the film was never found supposedly. Blue Book was strictly a cover-up program.

Cooper revealed he's convinced an alien craft crashed at Roswell, New Mexico in 1947 and aliens were discovered in the wreckage.

> I had a good friend at Roswell, a fellow officer. He had to be careful about what he said. But it sure wasn't a weather balloon, like the Air Force cover story. He made it clear to me what crashed was a craft of alien origin, and members of the crew were recovered.

Why has the government kept its UFO secrets for so many years? Cooper was convinced a lot of very embarrassed government officials are sitting there in Washington trying to figure a way to bring the truth out. They know it's got to come out one day, and I'm sure it will.

America Has a Right to Know!

Astronaut Gordon Cooper was one of the brave men who dared to expose the government cover-up of UFOs. *USA Today's* article on Gordon Cooper included this in the final paragraph:

> Cooper also authored the 2000 book *Leap of Faith,* in which he discussed NASA's early days, his experiences on the Mercury and Gemini missions and his belief in extraterrestrial intelligence. Cooper, in the book, said that as an Air Force pilot in 1951 that he chased UFOs while based in Germany.

The *Los Angeles Times* and *Chicago Tribune* included this quote,

> In the book, Cooper also embarrassed some of his old NASA colleagues with tales of UFO encounters and conspiracy theories. Claiming that film that he shot from Gemini 5 had been confiscated, he quoted President Johnson telling him, "Son, I ordered it classified."

The fact that CNN, *USA Today, Los Angeles Times,* and others reported this information is a significant shift from the past lack of reporting on UFOs. It is time for us to prepare the people of this planet to become a part of the galactic community. They are waiting for us to stop trying to kill each other before they invite us to join the community.

20

Understanding UFO Secrecy

It has not been difficult to make a compelling case for the reality of UFOs. The evidence is clear and overwhelming regarding this subject. The challenge is to make clear the reason for secrecy in relationships to UFOs. But the greatest challenge is explaining the "why."

1. Why all the secrecy?

2. Why a "black op"?

3. Why the unacknowledged government within the government?

4. Why hide the UFO/ET subject from public view?

The "why," the reason behind the secrecy, is the most challenging problem of all. There is not an answer to this question, but rather multiple reasons for such extraordinary secrecy. The reasons range from the fairly obvious and straight forward to the really bizarre.

Let's look at some key points regarding this secrecy, why it has been imposed and why it is so difficult for the controlling interests within covert programs to reverse policy and allow disclosure.

First let's understand the definition of "secrecy."

1. The act of keeping information secret

2. The quality or state of being hidden or secret

And according to another source, governments often attempt to conceal information from other governments and the public. These state secrets can include:

- Weapon designs

- Military plans

- Diplomatic negotiation tactics

- Secrets obtained illicitly from others ("intelligence")

Most nations have some form of Official Secrets Act (the Espionage Act in the US) and classify material according to the level of protection needed. An individual needs a security clearance for access and other protection methods, such as keeping documents in a safe, are stipulated.

Many countries have laws that attempt to limit government secrecy, such as the US Freedom of Information Act and sunshine laws. Government officials sometimes leak information they are supposed to keep secret.

Some will argue that secrecy is impermissible, as against the public in the area of elections where the government gets all of its power and taxing authority. In any event, permissible secrecy varies significantly with the context involved.

In the early days of the ET/UFO phenomena, military, intelligence, and industrial interests had concerns regarding the nature of this phenomena, whether it originated from our human adversaries and once it was determined to be extraterrestrial, how the public would react. Remember the radio show *War of the Worlds* the government is trying to prevent this action from occurring.

Once a phenomenon was determined to be extraterrestrial, there were many more questions than answers. Questions like:

1. Why are they here?

2. What are their intentions?

3. How do the devices travel at such fantastic speeds and through the vastness of space?

4. How might these technologies be applied to the human situation, in war and in peace?

5. How would the public react to this knowledge?

6. What effect would the disclosure of these facts have on human belief systems such as political, religious, and social systems?

Here is an example of how the public reacted on Sunday, October 30, 1938. Carl Phillips reported what he witnessed:

Ladies and gentlemen, this is the most terrifying thing I have ever witnessed. ... Wait a minute! Someone's crawling. Someone or ... something. I can see peering out of that black hole two luminous disks ... are they eyes? It might be a face. It might be ... good heavens, something's wriggling out of the shadow like a gray snake. Now it's another one, and another one, and another one. They look like tentacles to me. There, I can see the thing's body. It's large as a bear and it glistens like wet leather. But that face, it ... Ladies and gentlemen, it's indescribable. I can hardly force myself to keep looking at it, it's so awful. The eyes are black and gleam like a serpent's. The mouth is kind of V-shaped with saliva dripping from its rimless lips that seem to quiver and pulsate.

Carl Phillips continued to describe what he saw. Then, the invaders took out a weapon. A humped shape is rising out of the pit.

I can make out a small beam of light against a mirror. What's that? There's a jet of flame springing from the mirror, and it leaps right at the advancing men. It strikes them head on! Good Lord, they're turning into flame! Now the whole field's caught fire. The woods ... the barns ... the gas tanks of automobiles ... it's spreading everywhere. It's coming this way. About twenty yards to my right...

Then silence. A few minutes later, an announcer interrupts:

Ladies and gentlemen, I have just been handed a message that came in from Grovers Mill by telephone. Just one moment please. At least forty people, including six state troopers, lie dead in a field east of the village of Grovers Mill, their bodies burned and distorted beyond all possible recognition.

The audience is stunned by this news. But the situation soon gets worse. They are told that the state militia is mobilizing, with 7,000 men, and they are surrounding the metal object. They, too, are soon obliterated by the "heat ray." The "Secretary of the Interior," who sounds like President Franklin Roosevelt (purposely), addresses the nation. The radio reports that the US Army is engaged. The announcer declares that New York City is being evacuated. The program continues, but many radio listeners are already panicked.

What the radio listeners heard was a portion of Orson Welles' adaptation of the well-known book, *War of the Worlds* by H. G. Wells. Many of the listeners believed what they heard on the radio was real.

The Panic

Though the program began with the announcement that it was a story based on a novel and there were several announcements during the program that reiterated that this was just a story, many listeners didn't tune in long enough to hear them. Most of the radio listeners had been intently listening to their favorite program, the *Chase and Sanborn Hour* and turned the dial, like they did every Sunday, during the musical section of the show around 8:12. Usually, listeners turned back to the *Chase and Sanborn Hour* when they thought the musical section of the program was over.

However, on this particular evening they were shocked to hear another station carrying news alerts warning of an invasion of Martians attacking Earth. Not hearing the introduction of the play and listening to the authoritative and real sounding commentary and interviews, many believed it to be real.

All across the United States, listeners reacted. Thousands of people called radio stations, police, and newspapers. Many in the New England area loaded up their cars and fled their homes. In other areas, people went to churches to pray. People improvised gas masks. Miscarriages and early births were reported. Deaths, too, were reported but never confirmed. Many people were hysterical. They thought the end was near. Hours after the program had ended and listeners had realized that the Martian invasion was not real, the public was outraged that Orson Welles had tried to fool them. Many people sued. Others wondered if Welles had caused the panic on purpose.

The power of radio had fooled the listeners. They had become accustomed to believing everything they heard on the radio, without questioning it. Now they had learned – the hard way.

By the Eisenhower era, the UFO/ET projects were increasingly compartmented away from legal, constitutional chain-of-command oversight and control. This means that while we know from witness testimony that Eisenhower knew of the ET craft, the president (and similar leaders in the UK and elsewhere) were increasingly left out of the loop. Such senior elected and appointed leaders were confronted with (as Eisenhower called it) a sophisticated military-industrial complex with labyrinthine compartmented projects which were more and more out of their control and oversight. From direct witness testimony we know that Eisenhower, Kennedy, Carter, and Clinton were frustrated in their attempts to penetrate such projects.

This is also true of senior congressional leaders and investigators, foreign leaders, and UN leadership. This is indeed an equal opportunity exclusion project, it does not matter how high your rank or office; if you are not deemed necessary to the project, you are not going to know about it, period.

While there has been continued confusion in some covert circles over the ultimate purpose behind the ET phenomena, we know of no knowledgeable insiders who regard the ETs as a hostile threat.

By the 1960s, and certainly by the 1990s, the world was very familiar with the concept of space travel and the popular science fiction industry had thoroughly indoctrinated the masses with the idea of ETs from far away being a possibility, so why the continued secrecy? People would hardly be shocked to find out that we are not alone in the universe (the majority of people already believe this; in fact, most people believe the UFOs are real). Besides, what could be more shocking than to live through the latter half of the 20th century with thousands of hydrogen bombs aimed at every major city in the world? If we can handle that, surely we can handle the idea that ETs are real. The facile explanations of fear, panic, shock and the like do not justify a level of secrecy so deep that even the President and his CIA Director could be denied access to the information.

A Current Estimate

Continued secrecy on the UFO subject must be related to on-going anxiety related to the essential power dynamics of the world and how such a disclosure would impact these. That is, the knowledge related to UFOs/ET phenomena must have such great potential for changing the status quo that its continued suppression is deemed essential, at all costs.

Going back to the early 1950s, we have found that the basic technology and physics behind these ET spacecraft were discovered through very intensive reverse-engineering projects. It was precisely at this point that the decision was made to increase the secrecy to an unprecedented level, one which essentially took the matter out of ordinary government chain of command control as we know it. Why? Aside from the possible use of such knowledge by US/UK adversaries during the Cold War, it was immediately recognized that these devices were not your dad's Oldsmobile. The basic physics behind the energy generation and propulsion systems were such that they could easily replace all existing energy generation and propulsion systems on the Earth.

The disclosure of the existence of ETs, with the inevitable disclosure related to these new technologies soon to follow, would change the world forever and they knew it. This was to be avoided at all costs.

The technological discoveries of the 1950s resulting from the reverse-engineering of extraterrestrial craft could have enabled us to completely transform the world economic, social, technological, and environmental situation. And make no mistake, the changes would be immense.

To end the secrecy, means vast and profound changes in virtually every aspect of human existence economic, social, technological, philosophical, and geo-political. But to continue the secrecy and the suppression of these new energy and propulsion technologies means something far more destabilizing: the collapse of the Earth's ecosystem and the certain depletion of the fossil fuels on which we depend. There are no more generations to which we can pass this cosmic hot potato: We must deal with it and do what should have been done in 1950.

Remember, the entity which controls the UFO matter and its related technologies has more power than any single government in the world or any single identified world leader. That such a situation could arise was forewarned by President Eisenhower when, in January 1961, he cautioned us regarding the growing "military-industrial complex." This was his last speech to the world as president and he was warning us directly of a frightening situation about which he had personal knowledge. For Eisenhower had seen the ET craft and deceased ET bodies. He knew of the covert programs dealing with the situation. But he also knew that he had lost control of these projects and that they were lying to him about the extent and full nature of their research and development activities.

How would the world react to the knowledge that trillions of dollars have been spent on unauthorized, unconstitutional projects over the years? And that these tax-payer dollars have been used by corporate partners in this secrecy to develop spinoff technologies based on the study of ET objects which were later patented and used in highly profitable technologies?

Not only have the taxpayers been defrauded, they have then been made to pay a premium for such breakthroughs which were the result of research paid for by them! While the basic energy generation and propulsion technologies have been withheld, these corporate partners have profited wildly from other breakthroughs and benefits in electronics, miniaturization, and related areas. Such covert technology transfers constitute a multi-trillion dollar theft of technologies which really should be public domain since taxpayers have paid for it.

And how would the public react to the fact that the multi-billion dollar space program, using internal combustion rockets and the like, has been a primitive and unnecessary experiment since much more advanced technologies and propulsion systems were in existence before we ever went to the moon?

NASA has been as much a victim of this secrecy as have the rest of the government and the public. Only a small, very compartmentalized fraction of NASA people know of the real ET technologies hidden away in these projects.

Remember, covert reverse-engineering projects have resulted in huge quantum leaps forward in technologies that, once applied to military systems, could be a real threat to ETs, which may be here peacefully. The attempts to rapidly militarize space are likely a result of a myopic, militaristic, and paranoid view of extraterrestrial projects and intentions. If left unchecked, it can only result in catastrophe.

The reasons for secrecy are clear: global power, economic and technological control, and so forth. There are no easy choices. But there is one right one.

Department of Defense Memos Regarding Peru UFO

Covers Chapter 2

DEPARTMENT OF DEFENSE
Joint Chief of Staff
Message Center

Subject: IR 6 876 0146 80 (U)
THIS IS AN INFO REPORT, NOT A FINAL EVAL INTEL
1. (U) CTRY: PERU (PE)
2. TITLE (U) UFO SITED IN PERU (U)
3. (U) DATE OF INFO 800510
4. (U) ORIG: USDAO AIR LIMA PERU
5. (U) REQ REFS: Z-D13-PE030
6. (U) SOURCE: 6 876 0138 OFFICER IN THE PERUVIAN AIR FORCE WHO OBSERVED THE EVENT AND IS IN A POSITION TO BE PARTY TO THE CONVERSATION CONCERNING THE EVENT, SOURCE HAS REPORTED RELIABLY IN THE PAST.
7. -----ON DIFFERENT OCCASIONS NEAR PERUVIAN AIR FORCE (FAP) BASE IN SOUTHERN PERU. THE FAP TRIED TO INTERCEPT AND DESTROY THE UFO. BUT WITHOUT SUCCESS

PAGE 1

DEPARTMENT OF DEFENSE RECEIVED
JOINT CHIEFS OF STAFF
MESSAGE CENTER
JUN -3 1980

VZCZCMLT565
MULT
ACTION
    DTA:
DISTR
    IADR(01) J5(02) J3:NMCC NIDS SECDEF(07) SECDEF: USDP(15)
    ATSD:AE(01) ASD:PA&E(01) :IDIA(20) NMIC
-   CMC CC WASHINGTON DC
-   CSAF WASHINGTON DC
-   CNO WASHINGTON DC
-   CSA WASHINGTON DC
-   CIA WASHINGTON DC
-   SECSTATE WASHINGTON DC
-   NSA WASH DC
    FILE
(047)

TRANSIT/1542115/1542207/000152TOR15422=4
DE RUESLMA #4888 1542115
7NY CCCCC
R 0220527 JUN 80
FM USDAO LIMA PERU
TO RUEKJCS/DIA WASHDC
INFO RULPALJ/USCINCSO QUARRY HTS PN
RULPAFA/USAFSO HOWARD AFB PN
BT

SUBJ: IR 6 876 0146 80 (U)
THIS IS AN INFO REPORT, NOT FINALLY EVAL INTEL
1. (U) CTRY: PERU (PE)
2. TITLE (U) UFO SIGHTED IN PERU (U)
3. (U) DATE OF INFO: 800510
4. (U) ORIG: USDAO AIR LIMA PERU
5. (U) REQ REFS: Z-013-PE030
6. (U) SOURCE: 6 876 0138. OFFICER IN THE PERUVIAN AIR FORCE
WHO OBSERVED THE EVENT AND IS IN A POSITION TO BE PARTY
TO CONVERSATION CONCERNING THE EVENT, SOURCE HAS REPORTED
RELIABLY IN THE PAST.

7. _____ SUMMARY: SOURCE REPORTED THAT A UFO WAS SPOTTED
ON TWO DIFFERENT OCCASIONS NEAR PERUVIAN AIR FORCE (FAP) BASE
IN SOUTHERN PERU. THE FAP TRIED TO INTERCEPT AND DESTROY THE
UFO, BUT WITHOUT SUCCESS.

PAGE 1

DEPARTMENT OF DEFENSE

JOINT CHIEFS OF STAFF

MESSAGE CENTER

PAGE 2   18134
8A. _____ DETAILS: SOURCE TOLD RO ABOUT THE SPOTTING OF AN
UNIDENTIFIED FLYING OBJECT IN THE VICINITY OF MARIANO MELGAR AIR
BASE, LA JOYA, PERU (16805S, 071536W), SOURCE STATED THAT THE
VEHICLE WAS SPOTTED ON TWO DIFFERENT OCCASIONS. THE FIRST WAS
DURING THE MORNING HOURS OF 9 MAY 80, AND THE SECOND DURING
THE EARLY EVENING HOURS OF 10 MAY 80.
_____ SOURCE STATED THAT ON 9 MAY, WHILE A GROUP OF FAP
OFFICERS WERE IN FORMATION AT MARIANO MALGAR, THEY SPOTTED A
UFO THAT WAS ROUND IN SHAPE, HOVERING NEAR THE AIRFIELD. THE
AIR COMMANDER SCRAMBLED AN SU-22 AIRCRAFT TO MAKE AN
INTERCEPT. THE PILOT, ACCORDING TO A THIRD PARTY, INTERCEPTED
THE VEHICLE AND FIRED UPON IT AT VERY CLOSE RANGE WITHOUT
CAUSING ANY APPARENT DAMAGE. THE PILOT TRIED TO MAKE A
SECOND PASS ON THE VEHICLE, BUT THE UFO OUT-RAN THE SU-22.
_____ THE SECOND SIGHTING WAS DURING HOURS OF DARKNESS.
THE VEHICLE WAS LIGHTED. AGAIN AN SU-22 WAS SCRAMBLED, BUT THE
VEHICLE OUT-RAN THE AIRCRAFT.
8B. _____ ORTG CMTS: RO HAS HEARD DISCUSSION ABOUT THE
SIGHTING FROM OTHER SOURCES. APPARENTLY SOME VEHICLE WAS
SPOTTED, BUT ITS ORIGIN REMAINS UNKNOWN.
9. (U) PROJ NO: N/A
10. (U) COLL MGMT CODES: AB
11. (U) SPEC INST: NONE. DIRC: NO.
12. (U) PREP BY: NORMAN H. RUNGE, COL, AIRA
13. (U) APP BY: VAUGHN E. WILSON, CAPT, DATT, ALUSNA
14. (U) REQ EVAL: NO   REL TO: NONE
15. (U) ENCL: N/A
16. (U) DIST BY ORTG: N/A

BT
#4880
ANNOTES
JAL 117

PAGE 2   ORIG1111
NNNN
9222087

PAGE 2

8A. _____DETAILS: SOURCE TOLD RO ABOUT THE SPOTTING OF AN UNIDENTIFED FLYING OBJECT IN THE VICINITY OF MARIANO MELGAR AIR BASE, LA JOYA, PERU (16805S, 0715306W). SOURCE STATED THAT THE VEHICLE WAS SPOTTED ON TWO DIFFERENT OCCASIONS. THE FIRST WAS DURING THE MORNING HOURS OF 9 MAY 80, THE SECOND DURING THE EARLY EVENING HOURS OF 10 MAY 80.

SOURCE STATED THAT ON 9 MAY. WHILE A GROUP OF FAP OFFICERS WERE IN FORMATION AT MARIANO MELGAR, THEY SPOTTED A UFO THAT WAS ROUND IN SHAPE, HOVERING NEAR THE AIRFIELD. THE AIR COMMANDER SCRAMBLED AN SU-22 AIRCRAFT TO MAKE AN INTERCEPT. THE PILOT ACCORDING TO A THIRD PARTY, INTERCEPTED THE VEHICLE AND FIRED UPON IT AT VERY CLOSE RANGE WITHOUT CAUSING ANY APPARENT DAMAGE. THE PILOT TRIED TO MAKE A SECOND PASS AT THE VEHICLE. BUT THE UFO OUT RAN THE SU-22.
_____ THE SECOND SIGHTING WAS DURING THE HOURS OF DARKNESS. THE VEHICLE WAS LIGHTED. AGAIN AN SU-22 WAS SCRAMBLED, BUT THE VEHICLE OUT RAN THE AIRCRAFT.

BB. _____ OYRG CMTS: RO HAS HEARD DISCUSSIONS ABOUT THE SIGHTING FROM OTHER SOURCES. APPARENTLY SOME VEHICLE WAS SPOTTED, BUT ITS ORIGIN IS UNKNOWN.

9. (U) PROJECT NO. N/A
10. (U) COLL MGMT CODES: AB
11. (U) SPEC INST: NONE DIRC: NO.
12. (U) PREP BY: NORMAN H RUNGE , COL. AIRA
13. (U) APP BY: VAUGHN E WILSON, CAPT. , DATT, ALUSNA
14. (U) REG EVAL: NO REL TO: NO
15. (U) ENCL: N/A
16. (U) DIST BY ORIGI N/A

BT

D.O.D. Memo Regarding UFO Sighting

Newton's laws of motion are three physical laws that form the basis for classical mechanics. This can describe the relationship between the forces acting on one body and its motion due to those forces. They can be summarized as follows:

First law
Every object in a state of uniform motion tends to remain in that state of motion unless an external force is applied to it.

Second law
The relationship between an object's mass m, its **acceleration** a, and the applied **force** F is F = ma. Acceleration and force are vectors (as indicated by their symbols being displayed in bold font); in this law the direction of the force vector is the same as the direction of the acceleration vector.

Third law
For every action there is an equal and opposite reaction.

Therefore, a planet can be idealized as a particle for analysis of its orbital motion around a star.

B

Charles Halt Documents

Covers Chapter 6

Department of the Air Force
Headquarter 81st Combat Support Group (USAFE)
APO NEW YORK 09735

13 Jan 81

Reply to Attn of: CD

Subject: Unexplained Lights

To: RAF/CC

1. Early in the morning of 27 Dec 80 (approximately 0300L), two USAF security police patrolmen saw unusual lights outside the back gate at RAF Woodbridge. Thinking an aircraft might have crashed or been forced down, they called for permission to go outside the gate to investigate. The on-duty flight chief responded and allowed three patrolmen to proceed on foot. The individuals reported seeing a strange glowing object in the forest. The Object was described as being metallic in appearance and triangular in shape, approximately two and three meters across the base and approximately two meters high. It illuminated the entire forest with a white light. The object itself had a pulsing red light on top and a bank(s) of blue lights underneath. The object was hovering or on legs. As the patrolmen approached the object, it manoeuvred though the trees and disappeared. At this time the animals on

a nearby farm went into frenzy. The object was briefly sighted approximately an hour later near the back gate.

2. The next day, three depressions 1 1/2" deep and 7" in diameter were found where the object had been sighted on the ground. The following night (29 Dec 80) the area was checked for radiation. Beta/gamma readings of 0.1 milliroentgens were recorded with peak readings in the three depressions and near the center of the triangle formed by the depressions. A nearby tree had moderate (.05 - .07) readings on the side of the tree toward the depressions.

3. Later in the night a red sun-like light was seen though the trees. It moved about and pulsed. At one point it appeared to throw off glowing particles and then broke into five separate white objects and then disappeared. Immediately thereafter, three star-like objects were noticed in the sky, two objects to the north and one to the south, all of which were about 10 degrees off the horizon. The objects moved rapidly in sharp angular movements and displayed red, green and blue lights. The objects to the north appeared to be elliptical through an 8-12 power lens. They then turned to full circles. The objects to the north remained in the sky for an hour or more. The object to the south was visible for two or three hours and beamed down a stream of light from time to time. Numerous individuals, including the undersigned, witnessed the activities in paragraphs 2 and 3.

Charles I. Halt, Lt. Col. USAF
Deputy Base Commander

DEPARTMENT OF THE AIR FORCE
HEADQUARTERS 81ST COMBAT SUPPORT GROUP (USAFE)
APO NEW YORK 09755

REPLY TO
ATTN OF: CD   13 Jan 81

SUBJECT: Unexplained Lights

TO: RAF/CC

1. Early in the morning of 27 Dec 80 (approximately 0300L), two USAF
security police patrolmen saw unusual lights outside the back gate at
RAF Woodbridge. Thinking an aircraft might have crashed or been forced
down, they called for permission to go outside the gate to investigate.
The on-duty flight chief responded and allowed three patrolmen to proceed on foot. The individuals reported seeing a strange glowing object
in the forest. The object was described as being metalic in appearance
and triangular in shape, approximately two to three meters across the
base and approximately two meters high. It illuminated the entire forest
with a white light. The object itself had a pulsing red light on top and
a bank(s) of blue lights underneath. The object was hovering or on legs.
As the patrolmen approached the object, it maneuvered through the trees
and disappeared. At this time the animals on a nearby farm went into a
frenzy. The object was briefly sighted approximately an hour later near
the back gate.

2. The next day, three depressions 1 1/2" deep and 7" in diameter were
found where the object had been sighted on the ground. The following
night (29 Dec 80) the area was checked for radiation. Beta/gamma readings
of 0.1 milliroentgens were recorded with peak readings in the three depressions and near the center of the triangle formed by the depressions.
A nearby tree had moderate (.05-.07) readings on the side of the tree
toward the depressions.

3. Later in the night a red sun-like light was seen through the trees.
It moved about and pulsed. At one point it appeared to throw off glowing
particles and then broke into five separate white objects and then disappeared. Immediately thereafter, three star-like objects were noticed
in the sky, two objects to the north and one to the south, all of which
were about 10° off the horizon. The objects moved rapidly in sharp angular
movements and displayed red, green and blue lights. The objects to the
north appeared to be elliptical through an 8-12 power lens. They then
turned to full circles. The objects to the north remained in the sky for
an hour or more. The object to the south was visible for two or three
hours and beamed down a stream of light from time to time. Numerous individuals, including the undersigned, witnessed the activities in paragraphs
2 and 3.

CHARLES I. HALT, Lt Col, USAF
Deputy Base Commander

AFFIDAVIT OF CHARLES I. HALT

(1) My name is Charles I. Halt
(2) I was born on XXXXXXXXX
(3) My address is XXXXXXXXXXXXXXXX
(4) I served in the U.S. Air Force for 28 years, retiring in 1991 with the rank of Colonel. In December 1980, I was the Deputy Base Commander at the Anglo-American base, RAF Bentwaters, in Suffolk, England.
(5) Late in the evening on December 27th, and continuing into the pre-dawn hours of December 28th, in response to reports of unusual lights in nearby Rendlesham Forest, I led a team of USAF Security Policemen into the woods to investigate. This was the second such incident in as many days and rumors of UFO activity were rife on base. By going into the forest, my intention was find a logical explanation for mysterious lights.
(6) While in Rendlesham Forest, our security team observed a light that looked like a large eye, red in color, moving through the trees. After a few minutes this object began dripping something that looked like molten metal. A short while later it broke into several smaller, white-colored objects which flew away in a directions. Claims by skeptics that this was merely a sweeping beam from a distant lighthouse are unfounded; we could see the unknown light and the lighthouse simultaneously. The latter was 35 to 40-degrees off where all of this was happening.
(7) Upon leaving the forest, our team crossed a farmer's field. As we did so, someone pointed out three objects in the northern sky. They were white and had multiple-colored lights on them. At first, the objects appeared elliptical but, as they maneuvered, turned full round. They were stationary for awhile and then they started to move at high speed in sharp angular patterns as though they were doing a grid search.
(8) About that same time, someone noticed a similar object in the southern sky. It was round and, at one point, it came toward us at a very high speed. It stopped overhead and sent down a small pencil-like beam, sort of like a laser beam. That illuminated the ground about ten feet from us and we just stood there in awe, wondering whether it was a signal, a warning, or what it was. It clicked-off as though someone threw a switch, and then the object receded back up into the sky.
(9) This object then moved back toward Bentwaters, and continued to send down beams of light, at one point near the Weapons Storage Area. We knew that because we could hear the chatter on the two-way radio. Several airmen present later told me that they saw the beams. I don't remember any names at this point.

AFFIDAVIT OF CHARLES I. HALT

(1) My name is Charles I. Halt

(2) I was born on

(3) My address is

(4) I served in the U.S. Air Force for 28 years, retiring in 1991 with the rank of Colonel. In December 1980, I was the Deputy Base Commander at the Anglo-American base, RAF Bentwaters, in Suffolk, England.

(5) Late in the evening on December 27th, and continuing into the pre-dawn hours of December 28th, in response to reports of unusual lights in nearby Rendlesham Forest, I led a team of USAF Security Policemen into the woods to investigate. This was the second such incident in as many days and rumors of UFO activity were rife on base. By going into the forest, my intention was find a logical explanation for the mysterious lights.

(6) While in Rendlesham Forest, our security team observed a light that looked like a large eye, red in color, moving through the trees. After a few minutes this object began dripping something that looked like molten metal. A short while later it broke into several smaller, white-colored objects which flew away in all directions. Claims by skeptics that this was merely a sweeping beam from a distant lighthouse are unfounded; we could see the unknown light and the lighthouse simultaneously. The latter was 35 to 40-degrees off where all of this was happening.

(7) Upon leaving the forest, our team crossed a farmer's field. As we did so, someone pointed out three objects in the northern sky. They were white and had multiple-colored lights on them. At first, the objects appeared elliptical but, as they maneuvered, turned full round. They were stationary for awhile and then they started to move at high speed in sharp angular patterns as though they were doing a grid search.

(8) About that same time, someone noticed a similar object in the southern sky. It was round and, at one point, it came toward us at a very high speed. It stopped overhead and sent down a small pencil-like beam, sort of like a laser beam. That illuminated the ground about ten feet from us and we just stood there in awe, wondering whether it was a signal, a warning, or what it was. It clicked-off as though someone threw a switch, and then the object receded back up into the sky.

(9) This object then moved back toward Bentwaters, and continued to send down beams of light, at one point near the Weapons Storage Area. We knew that because we could hear the chatter on the two-way radio. Several airmen present later told me that they saw the beams. I don't remember any names at this point. From my position in the forest, it appeared that one or more beams came down near the WSA. At the time, the object was just to the north of the facility. I had great concern about the purpose of the beams.

(10) In keeping with official U.S. Air Force policy, I can neither confirm nor deny that the Weapons Storage Area held nuclear weapons. However, I am aware that other former or retired USAF Security Police who worked there at the time of the incident are now on-the-record confirming the presence of tactical nuclear bombs at the WSA.

(11) I believe the objects that I saw at close quarter were extraterrestrial in origin and that the security services of both the United States and the United Kingdom have attempted—both then and now—to subvert the significance of what occurred at Rendlesham Forest and RAF Bentwaters by the use of well-practiced methods of disinformation.

From my position in the forest, it appeared that one or more beams came down near the WSA. At the time, the object was just to the north of the facility. I had great concern about the purpose of the beams.

(10) In keeping with the U.S. Air Force policy, I can neither confirm nor deny that the Weapons Storage Area held nuclear weapons. I am aware that other former or retired USAF Security Police who worked there at the time of the incident are now on-the-record confirming the presence of tactical nuclear bombs at the WSA.

(11) I believe the objects that I saw at close quarter were extraterrestrial in origin and that the security services of both the United States and the United Kingdom have attempted—both then and now—to subvert the significance of what occurred at Rendlesham Forest and RAF Bentwaters by the use of well-practiced methods of disinformation.

(12) I have not been paid nor given anything of value to make this statement and it is the truth to the best of my recollection.

Signed: Charles Halt

Date: 6/17/10

Signature witnessed by: Katherine C. Shaw

Notary: KShaw My commission expires April 30, 2011

Seal:
KATHERINE C SHAW
NOTARY PUBLIC
MY COMMISSION NUMBER 284586
COMMONWEALTH OF VIRGINIA

Reference: http://www.dailymail.co.uk/sciencetech/article-1315620/US-airman-Charles-Halts-UFO-testimony-encounter-near-UK-nuclear-base.html

C

Rendlesham Forest
Incident

Covers Chapter 10

THE HALT MEMO

This is the text of the single-page memo written by Lt. Col. Halt to the UK's Ministry of Defense. It was on official US Air Force headed notepaper but was not classified in any way. The memo was released under the US Freedom of Information Act in June 1983 by the US Air Force to Robert Todd of the pressure group Citizens Against UFO Secrecy (CAUS). Note that the USAF had thrown out their own copy, evidently regarding it as of no further interest, and this copy actually came from the British MoD. The memo was dated 13 January 1981, over a fortnight after the events that are described had happened, and headed Unexplained Lights. The items in parentheses are all Halt's:

1. Early in the morning of 27 Dec 80 (approximately 0300L) two USAF security police patrolmen saw unusual lights outside the back gate at RAF Woodbridge. Thinking an aircraft might have crashed or been forced down, they called for permission to go outside the gate to investigate. The on-duty flight chief responded and allowed three patrolmen to proceed on foot. The individuals reported seeing a strange glowing object in the forest. The object was described as being metallic in appearance and triangular in shape, approximately two to three meters across the base and approximately two meters high. It illuminated the entire forest with a white light. The object itself had a pulsing red light on top

and a bank(s) of blue lights underneath. The object was hovering or on legs. As the patrolmen approached the object, it maneuvered through the trees and disappeared. At this time the animals on a nearby farm went into a frenzy. The object was briefly sighted approximately an hour later near the back gate.

2. The next day, three depressions 1.5 inches deep and 7 inches in diameter were found where the object had been sighted on the ground. The following night (29 Dec 80) the area was checked for radiation. Beta/gamma readings of 0.1 milliroentgens were recorded with peak readings in the three depressions and near the center of the triangle formed by the depressions. A nearby tree had moderate (0.05–0.07) readings on the side of the tree toward the depressions.

3. Later in the night a red sun-like light was seen through the trees. It moved about and pulsed. At one point it appeared to throw off glowing particles and then broke into five separate white objects and then disappeared. Immediately thereafter, three star-like objects were noticed in the sky, two objects to the north and one to the south, all of which were about 10 degrees off the horizon. The objects moved rapidly in sharp, angular movements and displayed red, green and blue lights. The objects to the north appeared to be elliptical through an 8-12 power lens. They then turned to full circles. The objects to the north remained in the sky for an hour or more. The object to the south was visible for two or three hours and beamed down a stream of light from time to time. Numerous individuals, including the undersigned, witnessed the activities in paragraphs 2 and 3.

(Signed)
Charles I. Halt, Lt Col, USAF
Deputy Base Commander

Postscript: In 2010, Dr. David Clarke revealed the previously undisclosed background to the Halt memo and the reaction to it at the MoD. Clarke interviewed Halt's boss Col. Conrad, the UK base commander Donald Moreland, and Simon Weeden who received the memo at the MoD UFO desk. The interviews confirm that the MoD made only a cursory investigation, not even interviewing the witnesses, and regarded the incident as of little importance. No further official report was made, or action taken, by the US or UK authorities beyond this memo. Halt has since claimed otherwise. But it is clear that he was not in a position to know.

Reference: http://www.ianridpath.com/ufo/appendix.htm

D

Lt. Gene Moncla UFO

Covers Chapter 14

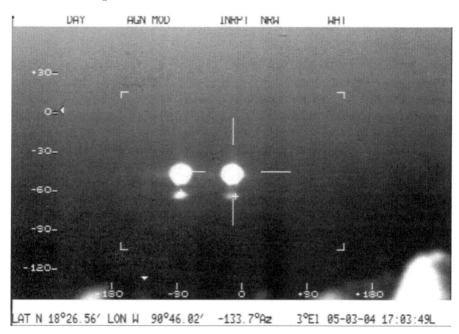

Two blips appear to merge, then both vanish

Note: This is an example only, not the actual image that was seen on their radar.

Newspaper reports of crash

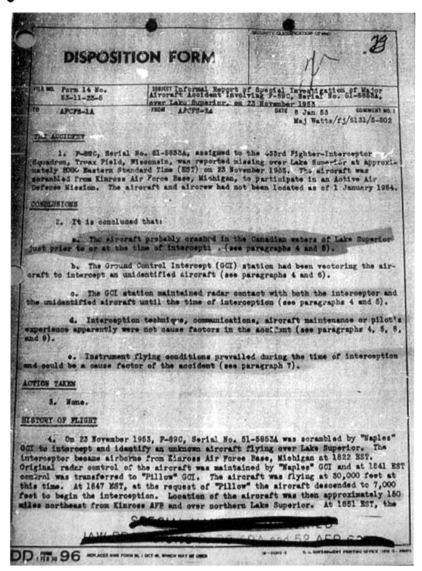

Form 14 - Informal Report
Form 14 - Page 1

DISPOSITION FORM	
FILE NUMBER Form 14 no. 53-11-23-5	SUBJECT: Informal report of a special investigation of major aircraft accident involving F-89C serial number 51-5835A over Lake Superior on 23 November 1953

THE ACCIDENT

1. F-89C, Serial No. 51-5853A, assigned to the 433rd Fighter Interceptor Squadron, Truax Field, Wisconsin, was reported missing over Lake Superior at approximately 2000 Eastern Standard Time (EST) on 23 November 1953. The aircraft was scrambled from Kinross Air Force Base, Michigan to participate in an Active Air Defense Mission. The aircraft and aircrew had not been located as of 1 January 1954.

CONCLUSION

2. It is concluded that:
   a. The aircraft probably crashed in the Canadian water of Lake Superior just prior to or at the time of interception (see paragraph 4 and 5)
   b. The Ground Control Intercept (GCI) station had been vectoring the aircraft to intercept the unknown aircraft (see paragraph 4 and 6)
   c. The CGI Station maintained radar contact with both the interceptor and the unidentified aircraft until the time of interception. (see paragraph 4 and 5)
   d. Interception techniques, communication, aircraft maintenance or pilot's experience apparently were not cause factor in the accident (see paragraph 4, 5, 8 and 9)
   e. Instrument flying conditions were prevailed during the time of interception and could be a cause factor in the accident (see paragraph 7)

ACTION TAKEN:

3. None

HISTORY OF FLIGHT

4. On 23 November 1953, F-89C, Serial No. 51-5853A, was scrambled by "Naples" GCI to intercept and identify an unknown aircraft flying over Lake Superior. The interceptor became airborne from Kinross Air Force Base, Michigan, at 1822 EST. Original radar control of the aircraft was maintained by "Naples" GCI and at 1841 EST control was transferred to "Pillow" GCI. The aircraft was flying at 30,000 feet at this time, At 1847 EST, at the request of "Pillow", the aircraft descended to 7,000 feet to begin the interception. Location of the aircraft was then approximately 150 miles northeast from Kinross AFB and over northern Lake Superior. At 1851 EST, the

Informal Report of Special Investigation of Major Aircraft Accident Involving F-89C
Serial No. 51-5853A, over Lake Superior, on 23 November 1953

Interceptor pilot was requested to turn to a heading of 20 degrees to the cut-off vector.
After the turn was completed, the pilot was advised the unidentified aircraft was at
11 o'clock, ten miles distant. Radar returns from both aircraft were then seen to
merge on "Pillow's" radar scope. The radar return from the other aircraft indicated
it was continuing on its original flight path, while the return from the F-89 disappeared from the GCI station's radar scope.

INVESTIGATION AND ANALYSIS

5. Radar reception was considered exceptionally good during the entire period
of the interceptor's flight. The GCI station was receiving the F-89's radar return plus
the F-89's Identification, Friend or Foe (IFF) return. At the time of interception,
when the target and the interceptor radar returns merged, the GCI controller first
assumed that the F-89 was flying formation with the other aircraft. This is normal
procedure when identifying an unknown aircraft. The simultaneous disappearance of the
F-89's radar and IFF return indicates the accident occurred at this time. If the IFF
had suddenly become inoperative then the regular radar return would continue to be
observed by the GCI operator. Both "Naples" and "Pillow" GCI stations reported difficulty in receiving radio transmissions from the pilot of the F-89 during the initial
period of flight. At one time, the pilot asked "Pillow" GCI if the intercept should be
discontinued because of the weak reception at "Pillow". He was advised to continue at
his own discretion. This radio difficulty was apparently temporary and probably due to
weather conditions. Later when the pilot was told to descend to the unknown aircraft's
altitude, the radio transmission was received loud and clear by "Pillow" GCI.

6. The unknown aircraft being intercepted was a Royal Canadian Air Force Dakota
(C-47), Serial No. VC-912, flying from Winnipeg to Sudberry, Canada. At the time of
interception it was crossing Northern Lake Superior from west to east at 7,000 feet.
This flight path was approximately 30 miles south of the intended flight path. The
pilot stated that he was on top of a 5,000 foot undercast and at the approximate time
of interception he was flying in the clear and visibility was unlimited. He also stated
he did not know he was being intercepted and that he did not see the F-89.

7. Weather conditions during the period of the interceptor's flight were marginal
and apparently deteriorated immediately after the time of interception. The Canadian
pilot of the aircraft being intercepted stated that, although he was in the clear at the
time of the interception, just prior to this he had been flying in instrument conditions.
Other pilots who took off to search for the missing F-89 reported various weather conditions but an analysis of all reports indicates definite instrument conditions with
snow showers in and around the Lake Superior area. Rime icing had been forecast for
this area and was also reported throughout this general area.

8. This F-89 was equipped with J35-A-41 engines which incorporates retractable
inlet screens. This would eliminate engine screen icing as a possible cause factor. The
aircraft had been previously flown for one hour on the day of the accident and the
pilot reported no discrepancies after the flight. The aircraft was then serviced and
returned to alert status. Technical Orders not complied with on the aircraft are not
considered as a cause factor in this accident. The aircraft weight and balance was
within limits at time of takeoff.

2

Form 14 - Page 2

Informal report of a special investigation of major aircraft accident involving F-89C serial number 51-5835A over Lake Superior on 23 November 1953

interceptor pilot was requested to turn to a heading of 20 degrees to the cut-off vector. After the turn was completed, the pilot was advised the unidentified aircraft was at 11 o'clock, 10 miles distant. Radar returns from both aircraft were then seen to merge on "Pillow's" radar scope. The radar return from the other aircraft indicated it was continuing on its original flight path, while the return from the F-89 disappeared from the GCI station's radar scope.

INVESTIGATION AND ANALYSIS

5. Radar reception was considered exceptionally good during the entire period of the interceptor's flight. The GCI Station was receiving the F-89's radar return plus the F-89 identification, Friend or Foe (IFF) return. At the time of the interception, when the target and the interceptor's radar returns merged the GCI controller first assumed that the F-89 was flying formation with the other aircraft. This is normal procedure when identifying an unknown aircraft. The simultaneously disappearance of the F89's radar and IFF return indicates the accident occurred at this time. If the IFF had suddenly become inoperative then the regular radar return would continue to be observed by the GCI operator. Both "Naples" and "Pillows" GCI Stations report difficulty in receiving radio transmissions from the pilot of the F-89 during the initial period of flight. At one time, the pilot asked "Pillows" GCI if the intercept should be discontinued because of weak reception at "Pillows". He was advised to continue at his own discretion. This radio difficulty was apparently temporary and probably due to weather conditions. Later when the pilot was told to decent to the unknown aircraft's altitude, the radio transmission was received loud and clear by "Pillows" GCI.

6. The unknown aircraft being intercepted was a Royal Canadian Air Force Dakota (C-47), Serial No. VC-912, flying from Winnipeg to Sudbury, Canada. At the time of interception, it was crossing Northern Lake Superior from west to east at 7,000 feet.

This flight path was approximately 30 miles south of the intended flight path, the pilot stated that he was on top of a 5,000 foot under cast and at the approximate time of interception he was flying in the clear and visibility was unlimited. He also stated he did not know he was being intercepted and that he did not see the F-89.

7. Weather conditions during the period of interceptions flight were minimal and apparently deteriorated immediately after the time of interception. The Canadian pilot of the aircraft being intercepted stated that, although he was in the clear at the time of the interception, just prior to this he had been flying on instrument conditions. Other pilots who took off to search for the missing F-89 reported various weather conditions but an analysis of all reports indicates definite instrument conditions with snow showers in and around the Lake Superior area. Icing had been forecasted for this area and also reported throughout this general area.

8. The F-89 was equipped with J35-A-41 engines which incorporates retractable inlet screens. This would eliminate engine screen icing as a possible cause factor. The aircraft had been previously flown for one hour on the day of the accident and the pilot reported no discrepancies after the flight. The aircraft was then serviced and returned to alert status. Technical orders not complied with on the aircraft are not considered as a cause factor in this accident. The aircraft weight and balance was within the limits at the time of takeoff.

2

Form 14 - Page 3

Informal report of a special investigation of major aircraft accident involving F-89C serial number 51-5835A over Lake Superior on 23 November 1953

9. The pilot and radar observer were assigned to the 433rd Fighter-interceptor Squadron, Truax AFB, Wisconsin. They were on temporary duty at Kinross AFB, Michigan, while the base's regularly assigned personnel were firing gunnery at Yuma, Arizona. The pilot had a total of 811:00 hours of which 121:40 hours were in F-89 type aircraft. He had 101:00 instrument hours and 91:50 hours night time. The radar observer was relatively inexperienced with a total of 206:45 hours of which 11:30 hours were at night. The medical history of the pilot and the radar observer is not considered as pertinent to the accident.

10. Search for the missing aircraft was conducted by both USAF and RCAF aircraft without success. Although 80 percent area coverage was reported, heavy snows precluded effective land search. All civilian reports of seeing or hearing the aircraft were investigated with negative results.

SUBSTANTIATIONS DATA ON FILE

IN THE DIRECTORATE OF FLIGHT SAFETY RESEARCH

11. The following substantiating data pertaining to special investigation of aircraft accident involving F-89C, serial number 51-5835A are on file at the Directorate of Flight Safety Research and can be obtained upon request:

A. Orders directing the investigation

B. List of personnel participating in the investigation

C. Statistical data

D. Missing Aircraft Report, Preliminary Report, Search Discontinuance Report

E. Form 14A, Pilot's Flight Records, Radar Observer's Flight Records

F. Pilot's activities prior to flight

G. Scramble Clearance, Weather

Informal Report of Special Investigation of Major Aircraft Accident Involving F-89C Serial No. 51-5853A, over Lake Superior, on 23 November 1953

9. The pilot and radar observer were assigned to the 433rd Fighter Interceptor Squadron, Truax AFB, Wisconsin. They were on temporary duty at Kinross AFB, Michigan, while the base's regularly assigned personnel were firing gunnery at Yuma, Arizona. The pilot had a total of 811:00 hours of which 121:40 hours were in F-89 type aircraft. He had 101:00 instrument hours and 91:50 hours night time. The radar observer was relatively inexperienced with a total of 206:45 hours of which 11:30 hours were at night. The medical history of the pilot and radar observer is not considered as pertinent to the accident.

10. Search for the missing aircraft was conducted by both USAF and RCAF aircraft without success. Although 80 per cent area coverage was reported, heavy snows precluded effective land search. All civilian reports of seeing or hearing the aircraft were investigated with negative results.

SUBSTANTIATING DATA ON FILE IN THE DIRECTORATE OF FLIGHT SAFETY RESEARCH

11. The following substantiating data pertaining to special investigation of aircraft accident involving F-89C, Serial No. 51-5853A, are on file in the Directorate of Flight Safety Research and can be obtained upon request:

a. Orders directing the investigation

b. List of personnel participating in the investigation

c. Statistical data

d. Missing Aircraft Report, Preliminary Report, Search Discontinuance Report

e. Form 14A, Pilot's Flight Records, Radar Observer's Flight Records

f. Pilot's activities prior to flight

g. Scramble Clearance, Weather

h. Statements, Ground Controller's Report

i. Accident Board Proceedings

j. Area map with Bogey's and Interceptor's positions plotted

k. Aircraft Engineering Data

JAMES I. CORNETT, Colonel, U. S. Air Force
Chief, Inves & Safety Engr Division

COORDINATION
Watts
Anderson
Alexander

H. Statements, Ground Controller's Report

I. Accident Board Proceedings

J. Area map with Bogey's and Interceptor's positions plotted

K. Aircraft Engineering Data

James I. Cornett, Colonel, U.S. Air Force
Chief, Inves and Safety Engr Division

S T A T E M E N T

When A-27-T was picked up by Pillow (P-16) it was believed to be
VC-912, but because the aircraft was off the flight plan course by about
30 miles, it was classified as "Unknown". Word was received from Naples
(P-66) that Horsefly wanted a correlation check on the track.

At 2317Z, Naples scrambled Avenger Red on a vector of 300° angels 30.
When the aircraft became airborne at 2322Z the pilot gave Naples a call
on channel 10 (UHF-2). Because their reception of Avenger Red was weak,
they attempted to pass control about 2335Z. At that time, we could read
Avenger Red only very faintly. Both "Receivers" and "Transmitters" at
this station were notified of the difficulty encountered in reading
Avenger Red, and checks of our equipment were made with no apparent
malfunction of equipment.

At 2341Z control of Avenger Red was passed to this station, although
the UHF reception at this station was poor. Avenger Red was, however reading our Transmissions about 4x4. Avenger Red was then directed to switch
to Channel 12 (UHF-1), and upon so doing it was learned that reception was
no better, whereupon both the fighter and this station returned to Channel
10.

About 2345Z Avenger Red asked if the intercept should be discontinued
because of the weak UHF reception at this station. The pilot was then informed that the continuance of the mission was up to his descretion.

About 2347Z Avenger Red was given a Port turn to 270 and was directed
to descend to angels 7. When Avenger Red answered with "Steady on 270",
he came in loud and clear at this station, and was informed of such. Shortly
thereafter, a clock and range report was given the pilot along with the

23 November 1953 A/C NO 51-5853A   Lt. Moncla

Lt. Stuart's Statement

STATEMENT

When A-27-T was picked up by <u>Pillow</u> (P-16) it was believed to be VC-912, but because the aircraft was off the flight plan course by about 30 miles, it was classified as "Unknown". Word was received from <u>Naples</u> (P-66) that <u>Horsefly</u> wanted a correlation check on the track."

At 2317Z, Naples scrambled Avenger Red on a vector of 300 degrees angle 30 degrees. When the aircraft became airborne at 2322Z the pilot gave Naples a call on channel 10 (UHF-2). Because their reception of Avenger Red was weak, they attempted to pass control about 2335Z. At that time, we could read Avenger Red only very faintly. Both receivers and transmitters at this station were notified of the difficulty encountered in reading Avenger Red and checks of our equipment were made with no apparent malfunction of equipment.

At 2341Z, control of Avenger Red was passed to this station, although the UHF reception at this station was poor. Avenger Red was however reading our transmission at 4x4. Avenger Red was then directed to switch to channel 12 (UHF-1), and upon so, doing it was learned that reception was no better, whereupon both fighter and this station returned to Channel 10.

About 2345Z, Avenger Red asked if the intercept should be discontinued because of weak UHF reception at this station. Then pilot was then informed that the continuance of the mission was up to his discretion.

About 2347Z, Avenger Red was given a Port turn to 270 and was directed and descend to Angels 7. When Avenger Red answered with "Steady on 270", he came in loud and clear at this station, and was informed of such. Shortly thereafter, a clock and range report was given the pilot along with the[...]

23 November 1953   A/C NO 51-5853A   Lt. Moncla

-2-

bogey's track and altitude. This information was acknowledged and the pilot
informed us that he was passing through angels 25. (Approx. 2349Z)

About this point, Avenger Red was informed that he might encounter
icing conditions on the descent to the bogey's altitude, such information
having been received from Horsefly. This transmission was acknowledged by
Avenger Red, who then asked for "Pigeons to Home Plate". Pigeons to Kinross
were given as 150 - 125 miles, which was acknowledged by the pilot.

At Approximately 2351Z Avenger Red was given a Starboard turn to 020 deg.,
which was the cutoff vector. About 2352Z Avenger Red was informed that the bogey
was at 11:00-10 miles, which was acknowledged by the pilot. Another clock and
range report was given, along with the information that the bogey was passing
from port to starboard, but no acknowledgement was received for either transmission. Just before the target merged on the RPI Scope, Avenger Red was
informed that he would be set up for another pass on the bogey if he had not
received a contact. When no answer was received from Avenger Red, it was
believed that his Radar Observer had established contact with the bogey on his
weapon and had taken over the intercept. Had such been the case, the Radar
Observer would likely have been keeping the pilot very busy — too busy to
acknowledge any transmissions. Thus, when there was no separation of targets
on the PPI Scope after the fighter had merged with the bogey, it was
assumed for a couple of minutes that Avenger Red was flying formation with the
bogey. Every few seconds, however, an attempt was made to contact Avenger Red.
When no contact could be established, Naples was contacted and advised to try
contacting Avenger Red. Naples efforts to contact the fighter were unsuccessful
also.

23 November 1953   A/C NO 51-5853A   Lt Moncla

-2-

[...] bogey's track and altitude. This information was acknowledged and the pilot informed us that he was passing through Angels 25. (Approx. 2349Z)

About this point, Avenger Red was informed that he might encounter icing conditions on the descent to the bogey's altitude, much information having been received from Horsefly. This transmission was acknowledged by Avenger Red, who then asked for "Pigeons to Home Plate". Pigeon to Kinross were given at 150 – 125 miles, which was acknowledged by the pilot.

At approximately 2351Z, Avenger Red was given a Starboard turn to 020 deg., which was cutoff vector. About 2352Z, Avenger Red was informed that the bogey was at 11:00-10 miles, which was acknowledged by the pilot, after clock and range report was given along with the information that the bogey was passing from Port to Starboard, but no acknowledgement was received from either transmission. Just before the target, merged on the PPI Scope, Avenger Red was informed the he would be set up for another pass on the bogey if he had not received a contact. When no answer was received from Avenger Red it was believed that his radar observer had established contact with the bogey on his weapons and had taken over the intercept. Had such been the case, the radar observer would likely have been keeping the pilot very busy – too busy to acknowledge my transmissions. Thus, when there was no separation of the targets by the PPI Scope, after the fighter had merged with the bogey, it was assumed for a couple of minutes that Avenger Red was flying formation with the bogey. Every few seconds, however, an attempt was made to contact Avenger Red. When no contact could be established, Naples was contacted and advised to try contacting Avenger Red. Naples efforts to contact the fighter were unsuccessful also.

23 November 1953 A/C NO 51-5853A   Lt Moncla

Lt. Gene Moncla UFO 137

-3-

Shortly after the two blips merged on the PPI scope, the IFF return
disappeared. It should be noted also that the fighter had been painting
a radar return on the scope in addition to the IFF return. Thus, it is
strange that no radar return on the fighter was picked up after the
merger, had the IFF suddenly become inoperative.

At the direction of Horsefly, two additional fighters were scrambled,
(Avenger Black and Avenger Purple) to proceed to the area of Avenger Red's
disappearance. At Naple's direction, Avenger Black gave several calls to
Avenger Red with the hope that contact might be established between the
two aircraft. When all attempts to contact Avenger Red proved futile
Avenger Black and Avenger Purple were vectored back to base by Naples.

When it became certain that the fighter was down, the Coast Guard
at Hancock was notified. They in turn called the District Headquarters
at Marquette to send out a Cutter from that station. Marquette then
called Houghton Radio to confirm the fact a fighter was down, and upon
receiving an affirmative answer, dispatched a Cutter for the area in
which Avenger Red is believed to be down.

/s/ DOUGLAS A. STUART
2nd Lt.,   USAF
Controller

A CERTIFIED TRUE COPY

DAVID C. COLLINS
Captain,   USAF
Aircraft Accident Investigating Officer

23 November 1953   A/C NO 51-5853A   Lt Moncla

-3-

Shortly after the two blips merged on the PPI Scope, the IFF return disappeared. It should be noted also the fighter had been pointing a radar return on the scope in addition to the IFF return. Thus, it is strange that no radar return on the fighter was picked up after the merger, had the IFF suddenly become inoperative.

At the direction of Horsefly, two additional fighters were scrambled, (Avenger Black and Avenger Purple) to proceed to the area of Avenger Red's disappearance. At Naples direction, Avenger Black gave several calls to Avenger Red with the hope that contact might be established between the two aircraft. When all attempts to contact Avenger Red proved futile Avenger Black and Avenger Purple were vectored back to the base by Naples.

When it became certain that the fighter was down, the Coast Guard at Hancock was notified. They in turn called the District Headquarters at Marquette to send out a cutter from the station. Marquette then called Houghton radio to confirm the fact a fighter was down, and upon receiving an affirmative answer, dispatched a cutter for the area in which Avenger Red is believed to be down.

DOUGLAS A. STUART
2nd. Lt.   USAF
Controller

A CERTIFIED TRUE COPY

DAVID C. COLLINS
Captain,   ASAF
Aircraft Accident Investigating Officer

23 November 1953   A/C   NO 51-5853A   Lt Moncla

27 November 1953

S T A T E M E N T

On the night of 23 November 1953 I was on duty as OIC of the 433 FIS alert detachment at Kinross AFB. At 1822 one 5 minute aircraft was scrambled, at 1915 a 15 minute aircraft took-off on a requested C.A.P., and at 1942 another 5 minute aircraft was scrambled leaving only one 5 minute aircraft on the ground. I called the control center and requested that they ask Naples to call down the C.A.P. so that we would have two 5 minute aircraft available. At that time I learned that one of the 5 minute aircraft had been lost by radar and radio and that the two aircraft that were airborne were trying to get radio contact with it. At 2007, the time when the lost aircraft would have been out of fuel, I notified Base Operations of an over-due aircraft, I also notified the Base C.O. of Kinross AFB, and tried to contact my squadron C.O., being unable to do so, I left the information with the 520th Group Operation Officer to be relayed to my squadron C.O.

At 2130 the C.O. of Kinross AFB suggested that I go to the area of last contact. I took-off and proceeded, under CGI control, to a point 75 nautical miles northwest of Kinross AFB where I had to return because of snow, showers, low ceilings and loss of radio & radar contact.

/s/ WILLIAM BRIDGES
Captain, USAF
AO2067460

A CERTIFIED TRUE COPY:

DAVID C. COLLINS
Captain, USAF
Aircraft Accident Investigating Officer

23 November 1953   A/C NO 51-5853A   Lt. Moncla

Capt. Bridges' Statement

On the night of 23 November 1953 I was on duty as OIC of the 433 FIS alert detachment at Kinross AFB. At 1822 one 5 minute aircraft was scrambled, at 1915 a fifteen minute aircraft took-off on a requested C.A.P., and at 1942 another 5 minute aircraft was scrambled leaving only one 5 minute aircraft on the ground. I called the control center and requested that they ask Naples to call down C.A.P. so that we would have two 5 minute aircraft available. At that time I learned that one of the 5 minute aircraft had been lost by radar and radio and that the two aircraft that were airborne were trying to radio contact with it. At 2007, the time when the lost aircraft would have been out of fuel, I notified Base Operations of an over-due aircraft, I also notified the Base C.O. of Kinross AFB, and tried to contact my squadron C.O., being unable to do so I left the information with the 520TH Group Operation Officer to be relayed to my squadron C.O.

At 2130, the C.O. of Kinross AFB suggested that I go to the area of last contact. I took-off and proceeded, under CGI control, to a point 75 nautical miles northwest of Kinross AFB where I had to return because of snow, low ceiling and loss of radio and radar contact.

WILLIAM BRIDGES
Captain, UASF
L02067460

A CERTIFIED TRUE COPY

DAVID C. COLLINS
Captain, USAF
Aircraft Accident Investigating Officer

23 November 1953   A/C NO 51-5853A   LT. Monck

Statement made by Lt. Mingenbach

STATEMENT

Lt Moncla and I had been on five minute alert on Monday afternoon 23 November 1953. The fifteen minute crews came on at 1700, stayed until 1745 and then left for dinner. They returned about 1815, and were about to takeover 5 min from Moncla and I when the scramble horn blew once and Lt Moncla was airborne about 1820. My R.O. and I left the alert hangars for dinner at 1825, returned about 1900, and I called Naples requesting a C.A.P. mission. Permission was received immediately and we were airborne about 1915. I called Naples on channel 10 at 1918 and was told to vector 330 degrees, angels 20, assigned call of Avenger Black, informed that radio & radar contact had been lost with Avenger Red and to attempt contact with him on channel 10. Until I was told to return to home plate my R.O. made a continuous attempt to contact with him on VHF channels I, 9, 10, 11, 1, and guard. During the climbout I encountered a broken ceiling at about 3000 feet, and subsequent layers of overcast to angels 20, where I requested an altitude change from GCI to angels 30. Permission granted I continued the climb and broke out above all clouds at angels 29. No icing encountered on climb. At about 1935, heading 330, altitude 25,000 my R.O. and I both believe we heard a short transmission from Avenger Red, recognizable as his voice, for about 5 seconds on channel 10. He seemed to be in the middle of a sentence when his transmission broke through, and therefore meaning was unintelligible. We called him back several times and received no reply. Shortly after this we were vectored 270, cruising at angels 30, and control was passed to Pillow.

My radio reception was very good, since I was clearly reading Naples vectoring Avenger Purple where I was 150 mi from home plate. Pillow vectored me over the area where contact had been lost by them with Avenger Red, and requested that I letdown in that area to investigate. Kinross weather had forecast moderate to heavy icing and snow showers for the local area, and since I was not sure that my anti icing system was operative, and did not have retractable engine screens, I hesitated to letdown into icing conditions that perhaps had given trouble to Avenger Red. Also snow showers combined with a low ceiling over the lake would have rendered effective search impossible in that area. I was informed that the request for me to letdown had come from Horsefly, and therefore Pillow nor Naples could do anything but have me orbit the area and continue to attempt radio contact with the lost aircraft. Finally, when Avenger Purple had come within 30

miles of my position, we were both told that Horsefly requested
we return to home plate and land. A normal letdown at Kinross
was accomplished under Naples control, light icing encountered
between 17,000 and 6,000 feet, and I landed at 2055.

WILLIAM MINGENBACH
Lt., USAF
A02234770

AS CERTIFIED TRUE COPY
DAVID C. COLLINS
Captain, USAF
Aircraft Accident Investigation Officer

23 November 1953 A/C NO 51-5853A Lt. Moncla

27 November 1953

S T A T E M E N T

On the night of 23 November 1953 I had the No. one ship on 5 min alert with the 433rd FIS detached to Kinross AFB, Mich. At 1942 Eastern we received a scramble order for one aircraft. I was airborne at 1946 and contacted Naples GCI on channel 10. My vector was 320° and 20,000 ft. I was assigned the call sign Avenger Purple and asked if my aircraft was equipped with retractable engine screens. I answered in the affirmative and was then told the purpose of the mission was to try to establish contact with Avenger Red. I was to letdown over the spot where contact was lost with Avenger Red and check for possible icing and also make visual or radio contact with the missing aircraft. On my climb-out I entered the overcast at 5,000 feet and although the clouds were in layers it was necessary to remain on instruments. When I reached 20,000 ft I was still on instruments and request an altitude of 30,000 ft which GCI approved. Approximately 120 miles from Kinross I was instructed by GCI to return to the field because the mission had been called off. During my letdown to Kinross light to moderate rime icing was encountered. I landed at Kinross without incident at 2050.

/s/ HOWARD R. NORDECK
2nd Lt.,   USAF
AO3004512

A CERTIFIED TRUE COPY:

DAVID C. COLLINS
Captain,   USAF
Aircraft Accident Investigating Officer

23 November 1953 A/C NO 51-5853A Lt. Moncla

Statement made by Lt. Nordeck

27 November 1953

STATEMENT

On the night of 23 November 1953. I had the No. one ship on 5 min alert with the 433rd FIS detached to Kinross AFB, Mich. At 1942 Eastern we received a scrambled order for one aircraft. I was airborne at 1946 and contacted Naples GCI. on channel 10. My vector was 320 deg. and 20,000 ft. I was assigned to call sign Avenger Purple and asked if my aircraft was equipped with retractable engine screens. I answered in the affirmative and was then told the purpose of the mission was to try and establish contact with Avenger Red. I was to let down over the spot where contact was lost with Avenger Red and check for possible icing and also make visual or radio contact with the missing aircraft. On my climb-out I entered the overcast at 5,000 feet and although the clouds were in layers it was necessary to remain on instruments. When I reached 20,000 ft. I was still on instruments and request altitude of 30,000 ft which GCI approved. Approximately 120 miles from Kinross I was instructed by GCI to return to the field because the mission had been called off. During my letdown to Kinross light to moderate rime icing was encountered. I landed at Kinross without incident at 2050.

HOWARD R. NORDECK
2nd. Lt.,   USAF
A03004512

A CERTIFIED TRUE COPY

DAVID C. COLLINS
Captain,   USAF
Aircraft Accident Investigating Officer

23 November 1953   A/C NO 51-5853A   Lt. Moncla

S T A T E M E N T

I talked to the pilot of the aircraft which was being intercepted by the F-89 #51-5853A at the time of the disappearance of the F-89. The Aircraft being intercepted was a Royal Canadian Air Force Dakota (C-47) on a flight from Winnipeg to Sudberry Canada. The pilot stated that the weather at the approximate last known position of the F-89 was an undercast with tops at 5000 ft. There was a scattered condition at 10,000 ft and above that the ceiling and visibility was unlimited. The pilot stated that he was flying at 7000 ft in the clear and visibility was unlimited. He stated that he had been in clouds during the earlier portion of his flight and that he had encountered moderate rime icing in the clouds.

The pilot stated that he did not know he was being intercepted and had not seen nor heard of the F-89. He stated that he heard no radio transmissions which could have emanated from the F-89. The pilot could offer no further information to throw any light on the investigation.

DAVID C. COLLINS
Captain,   USAF
Aircraft Accident Investigating Officer

23 November 1953 A/C NO 51-5853A Lt Moncla

Statement by RCAP Pilot

This statement by the RCAF Pilot of the C47 Intercepted by Moncla and Wilson's F-89 was written by Capt. David Collins, the USAF Aircraft Accident Investigations Officer.

STATEMENT

I talked to the pilot of the aircraft which was being intercepted by the F-89 #51-5853A at the time of the disappearance of the F-89. The Aircraft being intercepted was a Royal Canadian Air Force Dakota (C-47) on a flight from Winnipeg to Sudberry Canida. The pilot stated that the weather at the approximate last known position of the F-89 was an undercast with tops at 5,000 feet. There was a scattered condition at 10,000 ft. and above that the ceiling and visibility was unlimited. The pilot stated that he was flying at 7,000 ft in the clear and visibility was unlimited. He stated that he had been in clouds during the earlier portion of his flight and that he had encountered moderate rime icing in the clouds.

The pilot stated that he did not know he was being intercepted and had not seen nor heard of the F-89. He stated that he heard no radio transmissions which could have emanated from the F-89. The pilot could offer no further information to throw any light on the investigation.

DAVID C. COLLINS
Captain,   USAF
Aircraft Accident Investigating Officer

23 November 1953   A/C NO 51-5853A   Lt. Moncla

24 November 1953

Maintenance Report For A/C 51-5853A

Aircraft 51-5853A was given a thorough preflight inspection at approx. 07:30 on 23 Nov 53. No discrepancies were found during this inspection.

Aircraft 51-5853A was "scrambled" at 11:45 hours and returned at 12:45 hours. The pilots remarks in the AF Form I were Flt #1 "ok".

The A/C was immediately serviced and spot checked for worn tires, cleared engine intakes, oil, hydraulic tank levels, oxygen, nitrogen. All servicing caps and covers were securely replaced and the A/C was towed into the alert hangar where it was returned to number one aircraft on 5 minute alert status.

Th's aircraft was again scrambled at approx 18:15 hours without encountering any difficulty before take-off.

/s/ RAYMOND C. RICHARDS
T/Sgt, AF13162361
NCOIC 433rd FIS

A CERTIFIED TRUE COPY:

David C. Collins

DAVID C. COLLINS
Captain,   USAF
Aircraft Accident Investigating Officer

23 November 1953 A/C NO 51-5853A Lt. Moncla

24 November 1953

Maintenance Reports and Forms

24 November 1953

Maintenance Report for A/C/ 51-5853A

Aircraft 51-5853A was given a thorough preflight inspection at approx. 07:30 on 23 Nov 53. No discrepancies were found during this inspection

Aircraft 51-5853A was "scrambled" at 11:45 hours and returned at 12:45 hours. The pilots remarks in the AF Form I were Flt #1 "ok".

The A/C/ was immediately serviced and spot checked for worn tires, cleared engine intakes, oil, hydraulic tank levels, oxygen, nitrogen. All servicing caps and covers were securely replaced and the A/C was towed into the alert hangar where it was returned to number one aircraft on 5 minute alert status.

The aircraft was again scrambled at approx 18:15 hours without encountering any difficulty before take-off.

/s/
RAYMOND C. RICHARDS
T/Sgt, AF 13162361
NCOIC 433rd FIS

A CERTIFIED TRUE COPY

DAVID C. COLLINS
Captain USAF
Aircraft Accident Investigating Officer

23 November 1953 A/C NO 51-5853A Lt. Moncla

E

Major Robert White

Covers Chapter 17

On July 17, 1962, Major Robert White flew the X-15 to an altitude of 314,750 feet, or 59 miles, becoming the first "winged astronaut." He was the first to fly at Mach 4, Mach 5, and Mach 6; he was the first to fly a winged vehicle into space. After a career of "firsts," White died on March 17, 2010. White was one of the initial pilots selected for the X-15 program, representing the Air Force in the joint program with NASA, the Navy, and North American Aviation. Between April 13, 1960, and Dec. 14, 1962, he made 16 flights in the rocket-powered aircraft.

Source - http://www.nasa.gov/topics/aeronautics/features/robert-white.html

I have no idea what the objects were that I saw up there. I noticed a couple of particles first. They were very small, flaky objects. I thought they might be residue from the peroxide fuel that the engine burns. Then, I looked out the left window and saw what looked like a piece of paper about the size of my hand. It was about 30 or 40 feet away. It was grayish white, and I looked at it for a full five seconds before it moved away and I left it. I still don't know what it was.

Astronaut Gordon Cooper

Covers Chapter 19

Astronaut Gordon Cooper Mercury, Crew photo

Astronaut Gordon Cooper close up

Glossary of Terms

AGL
Above Ground Level

Altocumulus
A cloud larger and darker than those of cirrocumulus and smaller than those of stratocumulus. They are usually white or gray, and often occur in sheets or patches with wavy, rounded masses or rolls. They usually mean the development of thunderstorms later in the day.

CEFAA
Chili's Committee for the Study of Anomalous Aerial Phenomena.

CIA
Central Intelligence Agency.

CODA
Center for Operations of the Aerial Defence.

CNES
French Space Agency.

CODA
France Operational Centre of the Air Defense.

COMETA Report
English stands for "Committee for in-depth studies."

DIA
Defense Intelligence Agency.

DMCCC
Deputy Missile Combat Crew Commander.

DODIG
Department of Defense Office of Inspector General.

EMP weaponry
An electromagnetic pulse is a burst of electromagnetic radiation.

EVA
Extra-vehicular activity.

F-16
Nicknamed the Fighting Falcon, is a multi-roll jet fighter aircraft.

FAP
Branch of the Peruvian Air Force (Spanish: Fuerza Aérea del Perú).

GEPAN
National space agency of France, later named CNES.

JCS
Joint Chiefs of Staff.

LCC
Launch Control Center.

MoD
UK Ministry of Defence.

MUFON
Mutual UFO Network.

NARCAP
National Aviation Reporting Center on Anomalous Phenomena.

NATO
North Atlantic Treaty Organization.

NSA
National Security Agency.

OIFAA
Peru, Office of Investigations of Anomalous Aerial Phenomena.

P.A.F.
Peruvian Air Force.

Project Blue Book
United States Air Force investigation of Unidentified Flying Objects.

Radar Echo
An electronic signal that has been reflected back to the radar antenna; it contains information about the location and distance of the reflecting object.

RAF
Royal Air Force.

RCAF
Royal Canadian Air Force.

SAC
Strategic Air Command.

SEPRA
Formerly known as GEPAN (1977-1988) and SEPRA (1988-2004), is a unit of the French Space Agency CNES whose job is to investigate unidentified aerospace phenomena (UAP) and make its findings available to the public.

Taverny
An Air Base located in the communities of Taverny and Bessancourt France, twenty kilometers north of Paris. It is the headquarters of the French Air Force nuclear strike force, with an underground command center, and underground tunnels large enough for oversized vehicles.

UAP
Unidentified Aerial Phenomena.

UFO
Unidentified Flying Object.

Ufologists
Persons who study the UFO phenomenon.

References and Sources

1. http://en.wikipedia.org/wiki/Peruvian_Air_Force

2. www.af.mil/information/factsheets/factsheet.asp?id=188

3. "Encyclopedia of Associations," published by Gale Research

4. Former Air Force officers discuss UFO sightings – Air Force Times By Ledyard King – Gannett

5. www.freedomofinfo.org/national_press_07/santa_maria_statement.pdf

6. www.the-blueprints.com/blueprints-depot-restricted/modernplanes/sukhoi/sukhoi_su_22_fitter_f-26564.jpg

7. Carlos Santana Aguiar publication published: 3:08 p.m. 10/15/2010 *Inexplicata – The Journal of Hispanic Ufology*

8. www.freedomofinfo.org/national_press.htm

9. www.absoluteastronomy.com/topics/1976_Tehran_UFO_Incident

10. Wikipedia, the free encyclopedia

11. Leslie Kean "UFO's General, Pilots and Government Officials Go On Record"

12. Jim Klotz and Robert Salas

13. CUFON is dedicated to providing a free, 24-hour, public source of reliable, verifiable information. Since 1983, CUFON has been renowned as one of the few sources of excellent information on this phenomenon, as well as being a pioneer in the electronic media UFO information field.

14. www.theblackvault.com/wiki/index.php/Malmstrom_Air_Force_Base,_Montana (3-16-1967)

15. UFO Case Book

16. THE PRUFOS POLICE DATABASE by Gary Heseltine

17. UFO Conference – National Press Club, Washington D.C.

18. *Sunday Express* article on Belgium UFO. *Sunday Express*. 17 September 1995. Retrieved 21 March 2008.

19. "Report concerning the observation of UFOs in the night from March 30 to March 31, 1990 – ufoevidence.org." Retrieved 21 March 2008

20. Pierre Magain et Marc Remy, Les OVNI : un sujet de recherche? Physicalia Magazine, Vol. 15, n°4, pp. 311–318.

21. Original paper given to the French newspaper *Le Soir Illustré* and reproduced by "Les repas ufologiques parisiens" a french UFO association Le flou de bougé de la photo de petit-rechain par la calcul matriciel

22. Le Soir Illustré, Jean-Marc Veszely, Ovni: la retraite à cinquante ans? Belgian newspaper interviewing a mathematician about UFOs and the "photograph of Petit-Rechain"

23. Hallet, M. (1992). La Vague OVNI Belge ou le triomphe de la désinformation. Liège: Chez L'auteur

24. "The Belgian UFO Wave of 1989-1992 – A Neglected Hypothesis." Retrieved 9 January 2010

25. Abrassart, J-M (2010). The Beginning of the Belgian UFO wave. SUNLite, vol. 2, num. 6

26. Meessen, A. (2011). The Belgian Wave and the photos of Ramillies. The Belgian Wave and the photos of Ramillies

27. Paquay, R. (2011). Answer to "The Belgian wave and the photos of Ramillies." SUNLite, vol. 3, n°3

28. Printy, T. (2011). Questions about the Eupen UFO explanations. SUNLite, vol. 3, n°3

29. ufoevidence.org/cases/case1062.htm

30. freedomofinfo.org/national_press_07/duboc_statement.pdf

31. Claude Poher, GEPAN Report to the Scientific Committee, June, 1978

32. Dr. Claude Poher, Ph.D. in astronomy, founder and first director of GEPAN, the UFO investigative office under the French government's National Center for Space Sciences which analyzed reports from the Gendarmerie from 1974 through 1978, writing in the GEPAN Report to the Scientific Committee, June, 1978, Vol 1, Chapter 4.

33. "Col Halt's memo." Ian Ridpath. Retrieved 2007-04-13

34. "Transcript of Col Halt's tape recording." Ian Ridpath. Retrieved 2007-09-23

35. Col Halt's affidavit – differences from the original story

36. David Clarke. "The Rendlesham files." Retrieved 2010-09-29

37. "UK opens its own 'X-file.'" CNN. 2002-11-29. Retrieved 2007-04-18

38. "Ministers lift lid on UFO secrets." BBC News. 2002-11-28. Retrieved 2007-04-18

39. "Ministers lift lid on UFO secrets." BBC News. 2002-11-28. Retrieved 2007-04-18

40. hyper.net/ufo/rendlesham.html

41. Written by Dimitris Hatzopoulos

42. Taken from Nick Popes personal website

43. Ruppelt Edward, J. (1956). *Report on Unidentified Flying Objects*, DoubleDay

44. Jerome, Clark (1998). *The UFO Book: Encyclopedia of the Extraterrestrial*, Visible Ink Press

45. Maccabee, Bruce (2000). *The UFO-FBI Connection*, Llewellyn Publications

46. Transcript of Los Alamos conference

47. Ruppelt, Chapter 4

48. Menzel letter, May 16, 1949, cited at an Air Force Scientific Advisory Board meeting on the green fireballs in Washington, D.C., Nov. 3, 1949. The quoted section read, "Circumstances force me to conclude that the phenomena described are actually real. With regard to Dr. Kaplan's [meteor] explanation, which deserves very serious consideration, I merely raise the question as to why the phenomenon seems to be confined to the Alamogordo region."

49. For example, in contrast to his 1949 private statement to the Air Force that he didn't find the meteor explanation totally adequate, Menzel later wrote in his UFO debunking book, *The UFO Enigma* (1977), with Ernest Tavres that, "He and several other astronomers present observed the bright green object as it slowly traversed the northern sector of the heavens, moving from east to west: They quickly and unequivocally identified it as a meteor, or bolide..."

50. Robert Hastings, UFOs and Nukes, 2008, pp. 64-84.

51. Hastings, 64-70

52. Hastings, 70

53. Pflock, Karl T. Roswell: *Inconvenient Facts and the Will to Believe*. Prometheus Books, 2003

54. Steiger, pp. 132, 136

55. Blog listing modern green fireball reports from witnesses

56. Hall, Richard. "RCAF letter debunking AF claim." www.nicap.org. Retrieved 2009-03-02

57. NUFORC Case Brief

58. Aircraft Accident Board, USAF Accident Investigation Report for F-89 51-5853A, December 1953, Sect. "Findings"

59. Aircraft Accident Board, USAF Accident Investigation Report for F-89 51-5853A, December 1953, Sect. "Testimony of Lt. William A. Mingenbach"

60. Aircraft Accident Board, USAF Accident Investigation Report for F-89 51-5853A, December 1953, Sect. "Statement by Douglas A. Stuart"

61. Cherniack, David (2006). *The Moncla Memories* documentary film for Vision TV's *Enigma* series

62. Keyhoe, Major Donald E. (1955). *The Flying Saucer Conspiracy*, published by Henry Holt and Company, Pg.15.

63. Keyhoe, Major Donald E. (1955). *The Flying Saucer Conspiracy*, published by Henry Holt and Company, Pg.18

64. "Aircraft Parts Found in 1968." *Sault Daily Star*. Retrieved 2008-06-07

65. Carrion, James. "Update on Kinross/Great Lakes Dive Company." Retrieved 2008-06-07

66. Baillod, Brendon (August 29, 2006). "About Brendon Baillod's Great Lakes Shipwreck Research." northernexpress.com. Retrieved 2008-05-30.

67. Sachs, Harley L. (August 29, 2006). "Truth or Hoax...Disappearence [sic] of F89." northernexpress.com. Retrieved 2008-05-30

68. Staff. "To the moon and beyond," *The Record* (Bergen County), July 20, 2009. Accessed July 20, 2009. The source is indicative of the confusion regarding his birthplace. He is described in the article's first paragraph as having been "born and raised in Montclair," while a more detailed second paragraph on "The Early Years" states that he was "born Edwin Eugene Aldrin Jr. on January 20, 1930, in the Glen Ridge wing of Montclair Hospital."

69. Hansen, James R. (2005). *First Man: The Life of Neil A. Armstrong*. Simon & Schuster. p. 348. "His birth certificate lists Glen Ridge as his birthplace."

70. BuzzAldrin.com – About Buzz Aldrin

71. Solomon, Deborah; Oth, Christian (June 15, 2009 and June 21, 2009). "Questions for Buzz Aldrin: The Man on the Moon." *The New York Times*. Retrieved 2009-06-24. Note: nytimes. com print-view software lists the article date as June 21, 2009; main article web page shows June 15

72. From *The Dollar To The Moon*

73. "Brigitte Wambsganß, "Buzz Aldrin: Mond-Mann mit Trupbacher Wurzeln," Der Westen (Germany), July 17, 2009

74. RootsWeb's WorldConnect Project: Marc Wheat Database

75. "AdirondackDailyEnterprise.com Archives." [dead link]

76. Chaikin, Andrew. "A Man on the Moon." p. 585

77. *Life* Magazine. June 8, 1953. p.29

78. *Apollo Expeditions to the Moon*, Chapter 8, p. 7

79. Chaikin, Andrew. *A Man On The Moon*. p 204

80. (*First on the Moon – A Voyage with Neil Armstrong, Michael Collins, Edwin E. Aldrin Jr,* written with Gene Farmer and Dora Jane Hamblin, epilogue by Arthur C. Clarke, Michael Joseph Ltd, London (1970), page 251).

81. Hillner, Jennifer (2007-01-24). "Sundance 2007: Buzz Aldrin Speaks." Table of Malcontents – Wired Blogs (Wired). Retrieved 2007-05-07

82. "Webster Presbyterian Church History." Retrieved 2009-11-09

83. The Story of Tranquility Lodge No. 2000

84. Aldrin, Buzz (2009). *Magnificent Desolation: The Long Journey Home from the Moon.* Harmony.

85. Buzz Aldrin and Snoop Dogg reach for the stars with Rocket Experience, *Times* Online, June 25, 2009

86. America Movie Biographies [1]

87. Internet Movie Database [2]

88. "Buzz Aldrin Reveals Existence of Monolith on Mars Moon." C-Span. July 22, 2009

89. Aldrin, E. E., "Cyclic Trajectory Concepts," SAIC presentation to the Interplanetary Rapid Transit Study Meeting, Jet Propulsion Laboratory, October 1985

90. Byrnes, D. V., Longuski, J. M., and Aldrin, B. *Cycler Orbit Between Earth and Mars, Journal of Spacecraft and Rockets,* Vol. 30, No. 3, May-June 1993, pp. 334-336

91. Aldrin, Buzz (2003-12-05). "Fly Me To L1." *The New York Times.* Retrieved 2009-11-14

92. Aldrin, Buzz (2009-07-03). "Buzz Aldrin calls for manned flight to Mars to overcome global problems." *The Daily Telegraph.* Retrieved 2011-01-07

93. Roberts, Roxanne, and Argetsinger. "Love, etc.: Buzz Aldrin divorces; Hugh Hefner gets revenge on ex" (June 16, 2011). *The Washington Post*

94. "After walking on moon, astronauts trod various paths – CNN.com." CNN. July 17, 2009. Retrieved April 27, 2010

95. Read, Kimberly (2005-01-04). "Buzz Aldrin." About.com. Retrieved 2008-11-02

96. http://combatveteransforcongress.org/sites/default/files/2-26-10-invite.pdf

97. *Times* article: "10 Questions for Buzz Aldrin"

98. "Discovery Circumstances: Numbered Minor Planets (5001)-(10000): 6470 Aldrin." IAU: Minor Planet Center. Retrieved 2008-07-26

99. Personnel Announcements – August 22, 2001 White House Press Release naming the Presidential Appointees for the commission

100. [3] This sources states he was appointed in 2002, although according to the August 22, 2001 Press Release, it was 2001

101. "Variety International Humanitarian Awards." Variety, the Children's Charity. Retrieved 2007-05-07

102. Symposium Awards | National Space Symposium

103. Aldrin "Hollywood Walk of Fame database." HWOF.com

104. "Space Foundation Survey Reveals Broad Range of Space Heroes"

105. "BuzzAldrin.com – About Buzz Aldrin: FAQ". Retrieved 2008-06-09

106. Buzz Aldrin's Rocket Experience from Buzz Aldrin and FOD Team – Video

107. Making of Buzz Aldrin's Rocket Experience w/ Snoop Dogg and Talib Kweli from Buzz Aldrin, FOD Team, Ryan Perez, and Snoop Dogg – Video

108. "Astronaut Buzz Aldrin to dance with a different kind of star." Mother Nature Network. 2010-03-02. Retrieved 2010-03-03.

109. http://www.collider.com/2010/12/08/michael-bay-interview-transformers-dark-moon-edit-bay-visit/

110. Michael Kelly (2011). *Transformers: Dark of the Moon The Junior Novel.* Ballantine Little, Brown Books for Young Readers. ISBN 978-0316186292.

111. Comedy Central (June 6, 2011). "COMEDY CENTRAL's® *Futurama* Blasts Back Onto Your Telescreen All-New Episodes Begin Thursday, June 23 at 10 p.m." PR *Newswire.* Retrieved June 9, 2011

112. "Apollo 11 Mission Op Report" (PDF)

113. "NASA Ask an Astrobiologist"

114. Site containing a transcript of the UFO segment of the Untold Story documentary.

115. A link to The Science Channel scheduling info for cited documentary containing Aldrin's UFO comments

116. Morrison, David (2009). "UFOs and Aliens in Space." *Skeptical Inquirer* 33 (1): 30–31.

117. Schwartz, John (2009-07-13). "Vocal Minority Insists It Was All Smoke and Mirrors." *New York Times.* Retrieved 2009-08-11.

118. "Ex-astronaut escapes assault charge." BBC News. 2002-09-21. Retrieved 2008-09-03.

119. Steve Rock

120. *Knight Ridder* Newspapers

121. "Biographical Data: Mr. Deke Slayton." National Aeronautics and Space Administration. June 1993. Retrieved 2008-01-28

122. "Donald K. 'Deke' Slayton.' Wisconsin Aviation Hall of Fame. Retrieved 2008-01-28. "While at Edwards, Deke Slayton flew test flight missions on the F-101, F-102, F-105 and the F-106"

123. Kranz, Gene (2000). *Failure Is Not an Option: Mission Control from Mercury to Apollo 13 and Beyond.* New York City: Simon & Schuster. ISBN 0743200799. OCLC 43590801. "He was one of the hot test pilots at Edwards Air Force Base, pushing the F-105 to its limits"

124. History office, Peter W. Merlin, compilation done in 1998

125. "September 9, 1982: 3-2-1 ... Liftoff! The First Private Rocket Launch" by John C. Abell, *Wired* Magazine, September 9, 2009 http://www.wired.com/thisdayintech/2009/09/dayintech0909privaterocket/

126. "From Engineering Science to Big Science: The Collier as Commemoration." Retrieved 2011-02-10

127. "National Aviation Hall of fame: Our Enshrinees." Retrieved 2011-02-10

128. "Texas Oncology.com." Retrieved 2011-02-10

129. "Bobbie Slayton dead at 65." Retrieved 2011-02-10

130. "The Deke Slayton Memorial Space & Bicycle Museum." Retrieved 2011-02-10

131. *The Right Stuff*

132. *Apollo 13*

133. *Apollo 11*

134. *From The Earth to the Moon*

135. Source: Nov. 1988 issue (Vol 1, No. 3) issue of *UFO Universe* magazine; Condor Books 351 West 54th St., New York, N.Y. 10019

136. http://www.ufoevidence.org/documents/doc961.htm